AF556361

SOCIAL INTELLIGENCE OF STUDENT TEACHERS

SOCIAL INTELLIGENCE OF STUDENT TEACHERS

By

Kanikella Suresh

B.Com., M.Ed.

R.V.R. College of Education

Guntur, Andhra Pradesh

Editor

Dr. Digumarti Bhaskara Rao

M.Sc., M.A., M.A., M.Ed., Ph.D.

Reader & Research Director

R.V.R. College of Education

Guntur – 522006, A.P.

digumartibhaskararao@rediffmail.com

DISCOVERY PUBLISHING HOUSE PVT. LTD

NEW DELHI-110 002

First Published - 2009

Reprinted - 2015

ISBN: 978-81-8356-374-1

Social Intelligence of Student Teachers

Published by:

DISCOVERY PUBLISHING HOUSE PVT. LTD.
4383/4B, Ansari Road, Darya Ganj
New Delhi-110 002 (India)
Phone: +91-11-23279245, 43596064-65
Fax: +91-11-23253475
E-mail: discoverypublishinghouse@gmail.com
sales@discoverypublishinggroup.com
web: www.discoverypublishinggroup.com

Printed at:
Infinity Imaging Systems
Delhi

Dedicated

to

Mr. Tilak Wasan

Proprietor

Discovery Publishing House Pvt. Ltd.

in appreciation of his
service to education

PREFACE

Social intelligence means ability of an individual to react to social situations of daily life. It is the ability to get along well with others. It includes an awareness of situations and the social dynamics that govern them and knowledge of interaction styles and strategies that can help a person achieve his or her objectives in dealing with others. It also involves a certain amount of self-insight and a consciousness of one's own perceptions and reaction patterns.

The present study is intended to find out the level of social intelligence of student teachers. The student teachers studying in Colleges of Education are with a high level of social intelligence. There is no significant influence of gender, locality, teaching methodology, and qualification of student teachers on their social intelligence.

The student teachers with this high social intelligence can help the students in schools grow well in all dimensions of life along worth excellence academic achievement.

This study would be of great use to planners and administrators of teacher education and heads of teacher education institutions along with parents and society.

Dr. Digumarti Bhaskara Rao

Sri Sai Soudha
D-43, S.V.N. Colony
Guntur 522 006
A.P., India

CONTENTS

1

INTRODUCTION

Psychologists all over the world have made attempts to define intelligence in their best possible language but a definition which is universally accepted has not yet been noticed in any literature on intelligence. For example, intelligence has been defined as an ability of the individual. But, there is no agreement as to what kind of ability it is and the ability to do what like the blind men appraising the size of an elephant. Nobody seems to know precisely what intelligence is. It is worthwhile to quote some of the ideas here to arrive at an intelligent meaning of intelligence.

"Intelligence manifests in purposive direction, active adaptation and conscious correction. It is the ability to take and maintain a given mental set, the capacity to make adaptations for purpose of attaining the desired end and the power of self criticism." (Alfred Binet, 1916)

"An individual is intelligent in proportion to as he is able to carry on abstract thinking." (L.M. Terman, 1921)

"Intelligence is the global or aggregate capacity of an individual to act purposively, to think rationally and to deal effectively with his environment." (David Weschler, 1944)

"Intelligent is the analytic and synthetic ability of mind." (Charles Spearman, 1923)

"Intelligent activity consists of grasping the essentials in a given situation and responding appropriately to them." (A.W. Heim, 1970)

"Intelligence refers to a general level of cognitive functioning as reflected in the ability to understand ideas and to utilise abstract symbols (Verbal, mathematical or spatial) in the solution of intellectual problems." (D.P. Ausubel and F.F. Robinson, 1969)

Social Intelligence

In defining social intelligence one talks about a general category. The human capacity to understand what does happening in the world and responding to that understand in a personally and socially effective manner. One can not confine to this definition of social intelligence as it is not including within it all positive human attributes, making it a kind of definitional panacea.

What is trying to do in defining social intelligence is get at a quality in human beings which makes them capable of awareness and understanding in the broadest possible terms? Not mere financial or academic or interpersonal success but understanding which makes it possible to make their society better during their lifetime and after. Social intelligence is in the tradition of wisdom, not the more current idea of "smartness".

By defining social intelligence it is to create a new model for human behaviour and a new way of viewing reality. The model will attempt to get rid of truncated, lopsided definitions of intelligence, so one could no longer speak of a socially intelligent corporate CEO who takes American Jobs to Mexico and destroys vast parts of American life.

And the definition of social intelligence has to include such a person as Socrates, a man who ended his life as a condemned criminal but who achieved timeless success through passing on this understanding of what intelligence is the recognition of one's own ignorance and faithful dedication to one's principles.

Social intelligence is the ability to get along well with others, and to get them to cooperate with a person. Sometimes referred to simplistically as "people skills", social intelligence includes an awareness of situations and the social dynamics that govern them and knowledge of interaction styles and strategies that can help a person achieve his or her objectives in dealing with others. It also involves a certain amount of self-insight and a consciousness of one's own perceptions and reaction patterns.

From the standpoint of interpersonal skills, Karl Albrecht classifies behaviour toward others as falling somewhere on a spectrum between "toxic" effect and "nourishing" effect. Toxic behaviour makes people feel devalued, angry, frustrated, guilty or otherwise inadequate. Nourishing behaviour makes people feel valued, respected affirmed, encouraged or competent. A continued pattern of nourishing behaviour tends to makes a person much more effective in dealing with others; nourishing behaviours are the indicators of high social intelligence.

Social Intelligence and Personality

Social intelligence is one of the clusters of intelligences, according to the theory of multiple intelligences advanced by Howard Gardner of Harvard University. Gardner's 'Multiple Intelligences Theory' has become widely accepted in recent years, particularly in the area of public education.

The old idea that a person's potential in life can be measured and predicted by a single number — his or her IQ score - has lost a great deal of credibility during the last decade or so many. Researchers now accept Gardner's proposition that intelligence is multidimensional and many believe that each of the key dimensions of intelligence can continue to increase throughout one's life given the appropriate experiences, challenges and growth opportunities.

	Dimension	Involves
A	Abstract	Conceptual reasoning; manipulating verbal, mathematical and symbolic information
S	Social	Interacting successfully with others in various contexts.
P	Practical	Common sense capabilities; the ability to solve problems and get things done.
E	Emotional	Self-insight and the ability to regulate or manage one's reactions to experience.
K	Kinesthetic	Whole-body competence, e.g. singing, dancing, flying an airplane.

Gardner has proposed various categories of intelligence over the years of his research, typically, suggesting seven of them. In as much as he and others have recently been rearranging the categories and in some cases debating about how many intelligences we have. Karl Albrecht has taken the liberty of recasting them into a simpler model which is useful in business and professional settings. According to Karl Albrecht's simplified interpretation, we can think of human beings as having six primary dimensions of intelligence (A.S.P.E.A.K).

Measurement of Social Intelligence

Measuring social intelligence involves identifying key interaction skills and then assessing them behaviourally. All human interaction takes place with some context or other, and effectiveness involves mastering the contexts within which one is called upon to interact. So, according to this reasoning, social intelligence means understanding contexts, knowing how navigate within and between various contexts, and knowing how to behave in various contexts so as to achieve one's objectives. In other words, social intelligence is inferred from behaviour, so we use various observable behaviours as indicators of social intelligence.

Learning or Development of Social Intelligence

By first understanding social intelligence, as a combination of skill expressed through learned behaviour, and then assessing the impact of one's behaviour on others the degree to which one is successful in dealing with others one can experiment with new behaviours and new interaction strategies. In the simplest terms, this is the ability to "get along with people", which — it is a assumed — people learn as they grow up, mature, and gain experience in dealing with others. Unfortunately, many people do not continue to learn and grow as their age, and many people never acquire the awareness and skills they need to succeed in social, business or professional situations. It is quite clear that adults who lack insight and competence in dealing with others can make significant improvements in their social intelligence status as a result of understanding the basic concepts and assessing themselves against a comprehensive model of interpersonal effectiveness.

Social Intelligence and Emotional Intelligence (EI)

The recent popularity of the emotional intelligence concept one of Gardner's key intelligences paves the way for a practical approach to developing the other intelligences, while some practitioners have tried to stretch the Emotional Intelligence Theory to include "people skills". In practical terms, it makes more sense to think of emotional intelligence and social intelligence as two distinct dimensions of competence. Social intelligence (Gardner's Interpersonal Intelligence) is separate from, but complimentary to emotional intelligence (Gardner's Interpersonal Intelligence). We need both models in order to understand ourselves and the way we interact with others. Some deficits in social intelligence arise from inadequate development of emotional intelligence; conversely, some deficits in social intelligence may lead to unsuccessful social experiences which may undermine a person's sense of self-worth which is part of emotional intelligence.

According to Karl Albrecht, "I think of the six primary dimensions of intelligence, viz., abstract, social, practical, emotional, aesthetic and kinesthetic as analogous to the six faces of a cube. Each presents a distinct facet, or face, of one's total competence. We can think of them as separate for purposes of discussion and analysis, but actually they are intimately interwoven.

STATEMENT OF THE PROBLEM

A Study of Social Intelligence of Student Teachers.

NEED OF THE STUDY

Social intelligence is used to achieve social goals, resulting from any behavioural system. Social intelligence appears to be an important one of psychological abilities that relate to success in life. Social intelligence is empathy and communication skills as well as social and leadership skills that will be central to our success in life and personal relationship. Social intelligence helps one's knowing of social, identifying the social and self awareness. Social intelligence helps in understanding and analysing of others social intelligence. If we study the level of the social intelligence of student teachers, we can enhance it if found low, as it is one of the requisites of a good teacher.

SCOPE OF THE STUDY

The present investigation aims to identify the social intelligence of student teachers of Guntur district.

This investigation is limited to the variables gender, locality, qualification and methodology.

OBJECTIVES OF STUDY

1. To find out the social intelligence of student teachers.
2. To compare the social intelligence of male and female student teachers.
3. To compare the social intelligence of rural and urban student teachers.
4. To compare the social intelligence of graduate and postgraduate of student teachers.
5. To compare the social intelligence of Arts and Science methodology student teachers.

2

REVIEW OF RELATED LITERATURE

Any worthwhile research study in any field of knowledge requires an adequate familiarity with the work which has already been done in the same area. A summary of the writings of recognised authorities and of previous research provides evidence that the research is familiar with what is already known and what is still unknown and untested. Since effective research is based upon past knowledge, this step helps to eliminate the duplication of what has been done, and provides useful hypotheses and helpful suggestions for significant investigation.

Citing studies that show substantial agreement and those that seem to present conflicting conclusions helps to sharpen and define understanding of existing knowledge in the problem area, provides a background for the research project and makes the research aware of the status of the issue. Parading a long list of annotated studies relating to the problem is ineffective and inappropriate. Only, those studies that are plainly relevant, competently executed and reported should be included.
(Bhaskara Rao, Digumarti, 1997)

Capitalising on the review of expert researches can be fruitful in providing helpful ideas and suggestions. While review articles that summarise related studies are useful, they do not provide a satisfactory substitute for an independent research. Even though the review of related literature is not a substitute for an independent work, it is one of the first steps in the research process. It is a valuable guide to define the problem, to recognise its significance, to suggest promising data gathering devices, to appropriate the study design and sources of data for affective analysis and to arrive at fruit conclusions. (B. Veena Kumari and Digumarti Bhaskara Rao, 2000)

The search for related literature is a time consuming process, even though it is necessary, as earlier stated, for a good research work. Hence, this chapter review of related literature is meant for the study of related literature concerned to social intelligence.

Let us understand clearly the intelligence and social intelligence through the theoretical perspectives and research studies.

INTELLIGENCE

Intelligence, as a concept, has been understood indifferent ways by different psychologists and has, therefore, a wide variety of definitions.

Intelligence is the ability to adapt to one's surroundings. (Jean Piaget, 1952)

An individual is intelligent in the proportion that he is able to carry on abstract thinking. (Terman, 1921)

Vermon perceived three broad categories for defining intelligence. These were: (a) biological; (b) psychological; and (c) operational. Biological definitions emphasise the individual's capacity to adjust or adapt to environmental stimuli. Adoption, here, refers to modifying behaviour either overtly or covertly as a result of experience. Psychological definitions stress mental efficiency and the capacity for abstract thinking. Operational definitions involve making detailed specifications of intelligent behaviour and then finding measures of these specifications. Intelligent behaviour is thus expressed in terms of these measures. The expression "intelligence is what intelligence tests measure" is often used to describe the operational definition. (P.E. Vermon, 1960)

An analysis of various definitions reveals the following facts:

Intelligence is

1. The ability to profit from experience;
2. The ability to solve problems;
3. The ability to adjust and relate to one's environment;
4. The ability to perceive relationship;
5. The ability to think abstractly;
6. The ability to behave competently and effectively;
7. The ability to learn.

All these meanings are not mutually exclusive. Rather, they are interrelated. For example, if an individual can perceive relationship he can learn. If he can learn, he profits from experiences. This helps him to behave competently and effectively, to think abstractly and to solve problems. He is now able to adjust and relate to his environment.

Intelligence, as defined in standard dictionaries, has two other different meanings. In its most familiar meaning, intelligence has to do with the individual's ability to learn and reason. It is this meaning which underlies common psychometric notions such as intelligence testing, the intelligence quotient, and the like. In its less common meaning, intelligence has to do with a body of information and knowledge. This second meaning is implicated in the titles of certain government organisations. Both meanings are invoked by the concept of social intelligence. As originally coined by E.L. Thorndike (1920), the term social intelligence referred to a person's ability to understand and manage other people, and to engage in adaptive social interactions. More recently, however, Cantor and Kihlstrom (1987) redefined social intelligence as to refer to the individual's fund of knowledge about the social world.

E.L. Thorndike has classified intelligence into three categories which are as follows: (a) Concrete Intelligence; (b) Abstract Intelligence; and (c) Social Intelligence.

(a) *Concrete Intelligence:* Concrete intelligence means intelligence in relation to concrete materials. It is the ability of an individual to comprehend actual situations and react to them adequately; the concrete intelligence is evident from various activities of daily life. This kind of intelligence is measured by performance tests and picture tests in which the individual has to manipulate concrete materials.

(b) *Abstract Intelligence:* It is the ability to respond to words, numbers, letters, etc. All tests of intelligence which require manipulation of symbols are tests of abstract intelligence. Abstract intelligence is required in the ordinary academic subjects in schools, such as reading, writing, history and so on. The highest level of abstract intelligence is manifested in the thought of philosophers and in the use of mathematical formula.

(c) *Social Intelligence:* Social intelligence means ability of an individual to react to social situations of daily life. Social intelligence would not include the feelings or emotions aroused in us by other people, but merely our ability to understand others and to react in such a way towards them that the ends desired should be attained. High social intelligence is possessed by those who are able to handle people well. Adequate adjustment in social situations is the index of social intelligence.

SOCIAL INTELLIGENCE

Social intelligence is the ability to get along well with others, and to get them to cooperate with an individual. Some times referred to simplistically as "people skills", social intelligence includes an awareness of situations and the social dynamics that govern them and a knowledge of interaction styles and strategies that can help a person achieve his or her objectives in dealing with others. It also involves a certain amount of self-insight and a consciousness of one's own perceptions and

Psychometric View of Social Intelligence

The psychometric view of social intelligence has its origins E.L. Thorndike's (1920) division of intelligence into three facets, pertaining to the ability to understand and manage ideas (abstract intelligence), concrete objects (mechanical intelligence), and people (social intelligence). In his classic formulation: "By social intelligence is meant the ability to understand and manage men and women, boys and girls — to act wisely in human relations". Similarly, Moss and Hunt (1927) defined social intelligence as the "ability to get along with others". Vernon (1933) provided the most wide-ranging definition of social intelligence as the person's "ability to get along with people in general, social technique or ease in society, knowledge of social matters, and susceptibility to stimuli from other members of a group, as well as insight into the temporary moods or underlying personality traits of strangers".

By contrast, Wechsler (1939, 1958) gave scant attention to the concept. Wechsler did acknowledge that the Picture Arrangement subtest of the WAIS might serve as a measure of social intelligence, because it assesses the individual's ability to comprehend social situations. In his view, however, "social intelligence is just general intelligence applied to social situations" (1958) This dismissal is repeated in Matarazzo's (1972) fifth edition of Wechsler's monograph, in which "social intelligence" dropped out as an index term.

Defining social intelligence seems easy enough, especially by analogy to abstract intelligence. When it came to measuring social intelligence, however, E.L. Thorndike (1920) noted somewhat ruefully that "convenient tests of social intelligence are hard to devise.... Social intelligence shows itself abundantly in the nursery, on the playground, in barracks and factories and salesroom (*sic*), but it eludes the formal standardised conditions of the testing laboratory. It requires human beings to respond to, time to adapt its responses, and face, voice, gesture, and mien as tools". Nevertheless, true to the goals of the psychometric tradition, the abstract definitions of social intelligence were quickly translated into standardised laboratory instruments for measuring individual differences in social intelligence (for additional reviews, see Taylor, 1990; Taylor and Cadet, 1989; Walker and Foley, 1973).

Social Intelligence in the Structure of Intellect

After an initial burst of interest in the GWSIT, work on the assessment and correlates of social intelligence fell off sharply until the 1960s (Walker and Foley, 1973), this line of research was revived within the context of Guilford's (1967) Structure of Intellect model. Guilford postulated a system of at least 120 separate intellectual abilities, based on all possible combinations of five categories of operations (cognition, memory, divergent production, convergent production, and evaluation), with four categories of content (figural, symbolic, semantic, and behavioural) and six categories of products (units, classes, relations, systems, transformations, and implications). Interestingly, Guilford considers his system to be an expansion of the tripartite classification of intelligence originally proposed by E.L. Thorndike. Thus, the symbolic and semantic content domains correspond to abstract intelligence, the figural domain to practical intelligence, and the behavioural domain to social intelligence.

Within Guilford's (1967) more differentiated system, social intelligence is represented as the 30 (5 operations x 6 products) abilities lying in the domain of behavioural operations. In contrast to its extensive work on semantic and figural content, Guilford's group addressed issues of behavioural content only very late in their programme of research. Nevertheless, of the 30 facets of social intelligence predicted by the structure-of-intellect model, actual tests were devised for six cognitive abilities (O'Sullivan, et al., 1965; Hoepfner and O'Sullivan, 1969) and six divergent production abilities (Hendricks, Guilford, and Hoepfner, 1969).

O'Sulivan, et al. (1965) defined the category of behavioural cognition as representing the "ability to judge people". With respect to "feelings, motives, thoughts, intentions, attitudes, or other psychological dispositions which might affect an individual's social behaviour" (O'Sullivan, et al). They made it clear that one's ability to judge individual people was not the same as his or her comprehension of people in general or "stereotypic understanding" and bore no a priori relation to one's ability to understand oneself. Apparently, these two aspects of social cognition lie outside the standard structure-of-intellect model.

In constructing their tests of behavioural cognition, O'Sullivan et al. (1965) assumed that "expressive behaviour, more particularly facial expressions, vocal inflections, postures, and gestures, are the cues from which intentional states are inferred". While recognising the value of assessing the ability to decode these cues in real-life contexts with real people serving as targets, economic constraints forced the investigators to rely on photographs, cartoons, drawings, and tape recordings (the cost of film was prohibitive); verbal materials were avoided wherever possible, presumably in order to avoid contamination of social intelligence by verbal abilities. In the final analysis, O'Sullivan, et.al developed at least three different tests within each product domain, each test consisting of 30 or more separate items — by any standard, a monumental effort at theory-guided test construction.

The six cognitive abilities defined by O'Sullivan et al. were: (i) Cognition of behavioural units: the ability to identify the internal mental states of individuals; (ii) Cognition of behavioural classes: the ability to group together other people's mental states on the basis of similarity; (iii) Cognition of behavioural relations: the ability to interpret meaningful connections among behavioural acts; (iv) Cognition of behavioural systems: the ability to interpret sequences of social behaviour; (v) Cognition of behavioural transformations: the ability to respond flexibly in interpreting changes in social behaviour; and (vi) Cognition of behavioural implications: the ability to predict what will happen in an interpersonal situation.

After devising these tests, O'Sullivan, et al. (1965) conducted a normative study in which 306 high-school students received 23 different social intelligence tests representing the six hypothesised factors, along with 24 measures of 12 non-social ability factors. A principal factor analysis with orthogonal rotation yielded 22 factors, including the 12 non-social reference factors and 6 factors clearly interpretable as cognition of behaviour. In general, the six behavioural factors were not contaminated by non-social semantic and spatial abilities. Thus, O'Sullivan et al. apparently succeeded in measuring expressly social abilities which were essentially independent of abstract cognitive ability. However, echoing earlier findings with the GWSIT, later studies found substantial correlations between IQ and scores on the individual Guilford subtests, as well as various composite social intelligence scores (Riggio, Messamer, and Throckmorton, 1991; Shanley, Walker, and Foley, 1971). Still Shanley, et al. conceded that the correlations obtained were not strong enough to warrant the conclusion (e.g., Wechsler, 1958) that social intelligence is nothing more than general intelligence applied in the social domain.

In one of the last test-construction efforts by Guilford's group, Hendricks et. al (1969) attempted to develop tests for coping with other people, not just understanding them through their behaviour — what they referred to as "basic solution-finding skills in interpersonal relations" (p. 3). Because successful coping involves the creative generation of many and diverse behavioural ideas, these investigators labelled these divergent-thinking abilities creative social intelligence.

The six divergent production abilities defined by Hendricks, et al., were: (i) Divergent production of behavioural units: the ability to engage in behavioural acts which communicate internal mental states; (ii) Divergent production of behavioural classes— the ability to create recognisable categories of behavioural acts; (iii) Divergent production of behavioural relations—the ability to perform an act which has a bearing on what another person is doing; (iv) Divergent production of behavioural systems: the ability to maintain a sequence of interactions with another person; (v) Divergent production of behavioral transformations—the ability to alter an expression or a sequence of expressions; and (vi) Divergent production of behavioral implications—the ability to predict many possible outcomes of a setting.

As with the behavioural cognition abilities studied by O'Sullivan, et al. (1965), the very nature of the behavioural domain raised serious technical problems for test development in the behavioural domain, especially with respect to contamination by verbal (semantic) abilities. Ideally, of course, divergent production would be measured in real-world settings, in terms of actual behavioural responses to real people. Failing that, testing could rely on non-verbal behaviours such as drawings, gestures, and vocalisations, but such tests could well be contaminated by individual differences in drawing, acting, or public-speaking ability that have nothing to do with social intelligence per se.

Still, following the pattern of O'Sullivan, et al. (1965), a battery of creative social intelligence tests, 22 for divergent production of behavioural products and another 16 representing 8 categories of cognition of behaviour and divergent production in the semantic domain, was administered to 252 high-school students. As might be expected, scoring divergent productions proved considerably harder than scoring cognitions, as in the former case there is no one best answer, and the subject's responses must be evaluated by independent judges for quality as well as quantity. Principal-components analysis yielded 15 factors, with six factors clearly interpretable as divergent production in the behavioural domain. Again, the divergent-production abilities in the behavioural domain were essentially independent of both divergent semantic production and cognition in the behavioural domain.

A later study by Chen and Michael (1993), employing more modern factor-analytic techniques, essentially confirmed these findings. In addition, Chen and Michael extracted a set of higher-order factors which largely conformed to the theoretical predictions of Guilford's (1981) revised structure-of-intellect model. A similar reanalysis of the O'Sullivan et al. (1965) has yet to be reported.

In summary, Guilford and his colleagues were successful in devising measures for two rather different domains of social intelligence: understanding the behaviour of other people (cognition of behavioural content), and coping with the behaviour of other people (divergent production of behavioural content). These component abilities were relatively independent of each other within the behavioural domain, and each was also relatively independent of the non-behavioural abilities, as predicted (and required) by the structure-of-intellect model.

Despite the huge amount of effort that the Guilford group invested in the measurement of social intelligence, it should be understood that the studies of O'Sullivan, et al. (1965) and Hendricks, et al. (1969) went only part of the way toward establishing the construct validity of social intelligence. Their studies described essentially established convergent and discriminate validity, by showing that ostensible tests of the various behavioural abilities hung together as predicted by the theory, and were not contaminated by other abilities outside the behavioural domain. As yet, there is little evidence for the ability of any of these tests to predict external criteria of social intelligence.

Tests of the remaining three structure-of-intellect domains (memory, convergent production, and evaluation) had not developed by the time the Guilford programme came to a close. Hendricks et al. (1969) noted that "these constitute by far the greatest number of unknowns in the "Structure of Intellect] model". However, O'Sullivan, et al. (1965) did sketch out how these abilities were defined. Convergent production in the behavioral domain was defined as "doing the right thing at the right time" and presumably might be tested by a knowledge of etiquette. Behavioural memory was defined as the ability to remember the social characteristics of people (e.g., names, faces, and personality traits), while behavioural evaluation was defined as the ability to judge the appropriateness of behaviour.

Convergent and Discriminate Validity in Social Intelligence

Following the Guilford studies, a number of investigators continued the attempt to define social intelligence and determine its relation to general abstract intelligence. Most of these studies explicitly employ the logic of the 'multi-trait multi method' matrix (Campbell and Fiske, 1959), employing multiple measures of social and non-social intelligence, and examining the convergent validity of alternative measures within each domain, and their discriminate validity across domains (e.g., Sechrest and Jackson, 1961).

For example, Keating (1978) measured social intelligence with a battery of instruments including Rest's (1975) Defining Issues Test, derived from Kohlberg's (1963) theory of moral development; Chapin's (1942) Social Insight Test, which asks the subject to resolve various social dilemmas; and Gough's (1966) Social Maturity Index, a self-report scale derived from the California Psychological Inventory measuring effective social functioning. Applying a 'multi-trait multi-method' analysis, Keating found no evidence that social intelligence, so defined, was discriminable from academic intelligence. Thus, the average correlation between tests within each domain was actually lower than the corresponding average across domains. While a factor analysis produced two factors, each of these factors consisted of a mix of the two types of intelligence test. Finally, Keating found that the three measures of abstract intelligence were actually better predictors of Gough's (1966) Social Maturity Index than were the remaining two measures of social intelligence. However, it should be noted that Keating's putative measures of social intelligence are highly verbal in nature, so some contamination by abstract verbal and reasoning ability might be expected.

In response to Keating's (1978) study, Ford and Tisak (1983) conducted an even more substantial study involving over 600 high-school students. Four measures of verbal and mathematical ability were derived from school records of grades and standardised test scores. Social intelligence was measured by self-, peer-, and teacher-ratings of social competence, Hogan's (1969) empathy test, self-reports of social competence, and a judgment based on an individual interview. In contrast to Keating's (1968) results, Ford and Tisak found that the measures of academic and social intelligence loaded on different factors. Moreover, the three ratings of social competence and Hogan's empathy scale were more highly predictive of the interview ratings of social competence than were the academic measures. Ford and Tisak attributed these results to the selection of social intelligence measures according to a criterion of behavioural effectiveness in social situations, rather than cognitive understanding of them. Put another way: measures of verbal ability, including standard measures of IQ, are likely to correlate highly with verbal measures, but not non-verbal measures, of social intelligence.

Similar findings were obtained by a number of other investigators (e.g., Brown and Anthony, 1990), including Marlowe (1986; Marlowe and Bedell, 1982), who assembled a large battery of personality measures ostensibly tapping various aspects of social intelligence. Factor analysis of these instruments yielded five dimensions of social intelligence: interest and concern for other people, social performance skills, empathic ability, emotional expressiveness and sensitivity to others' emotional expressions, and social anxiety and lack of social self-efficacy and self-esteem. Factor scores on these dimensions of social intelligence were essentially unrelated to measures of verbal and abstract intelligence.

In evaluating studies like Marlowe's (1986), however, it should be noted that the apparent independence of social and general intelligence may be at least partially an artifact of method variance. Unlike the GWSIT, and the batteries of cognitive and divergent-production measures devised by the Guilford group, Marlowe's ostensible measures of social intelligence are all self-report scales, whereas his measures of verbal and abstract intelligence were the usual sorts of objective performance tests. The difference in data collection methods alone may explain why the social and verbal/abstract dimensions lined up on different factors. In any event, the measurement of individual differences in social intelligence by means of self-report scales is a major departure from the tradition of intelligence testing, and it seems important to confirm Marlowe's findings using objective performance measures of the various facets of social intelligence.

For example, Frederickson, Carlson, and Ward (1984) employed an extensive behavioural assessment procedure, along with a battery of performance tests of scholastic aptitude and achievement and medical and non-medical problem solving. In addition, each subject conducted 10 interviews with simulated medical patients and non-medical clients. Based on coding of their interview behaviour, each subject received ratings of organisation, warmth, and control. None of the measures of aptitude, achievement, or problem-solving behaviour correlated substantially with any of the interview-based ratings of social intelligence. Lowman and Leeman (1988), employing a number of performance measures, obtained evidence for three dimensions of social intelligence: social needs and interests, social knowledge, and social ability. Interestingly, the correlations of all three dimensions with grade point average, a proxy for academic intelligence, were either null or negative.

On the other hand, Stricker and Rock (1990) administered a battery of performance measures of social intelligence, and found that subjects' accuracy in judging a person and a situation portrayed in a videotaped interview was correlated with verbal ability. Wong, Day, Maxwell, and Meara (1995) constructed measures of social perception (accuracy in decoding verbal and non-verbal behaviour), social insight (accuracy in interpreting social behaviour) and social knowledge (awareness of the rules of etiquette). Factor analysis showed that social perception and insight were closely related, neither of these dimensions was closely related to social knowledge, and none of the social abilities was related to traditional academic ability.

Expanding on the study by Wong et al., Jones and Day (1997) based their analysis on Cattell's (1971) distinction between fluid and crystallised intelligence. In the social domain, crystallised intelligence reflects the individual's accumulated fund of knowledge about the social world, including his or her vocabulary for representing social behaviours and situations; fluid intelligence, by contrast, reflects the individual's ability to quickly and accurately solve problems posed by novel social situations. Jones and Day assembled four measures of each kind of ability, including verbal and pictorial performance measures, self-ratings, and teacher ratings. They also had multiple measures of academic ability. Confirmatory factor analyses testing various specific models of the relations between social and academic intelligence indicated that crystallised social intelligence was discriminable from fluid social intelligence, but not from academic intelligence.

Clearly, more studies employing performance-based measures are needed before any definitive conclusions can be drawn about the relations among various aspects of social intelligence (convergent validity) and the relations between social intelligence and other intellectual abilities (discriminate validity).

Social Intelligence as a Cognitive Module

An exception to the general rule that social intelligence plays little role in scientific theories of intelligence is the theory of multiple intelligences proposed by Gardner (1983, 1993). Unlike Spearman (1927), and other advocates of general intelligence (e.g., Jensen, 1998), Gardner has proposed that intelligence is not a unitary cognitive ability, but that there are seven (and perhaps more) quite different kinds of intelligence, each hypothetically dissociable from the others, and each hypothetically associated with a different brain system. While most of these proposed intelligences (linguistic, logical-mathematical, spatial, musical, and bodily-kinesthetic) are "cognitive" abilities somewhat reminiscent of Thurstone's primary mental abilities, two are explicitly personal and social in nature. Gardner defines intrapersonal intelligence as the person's ability to gain access to his or her own internal emotional life, and interpersonal intelligence as the individual's ability to notice and make distinctions among other individuals.

Although Gardner's (1983) multiple intelligences are individual-differences constructs, in which some people, or some groups, are assumed to have more of these abilities than others, Gardner does not rely on the traditional psychometric procedures - scale construction, factor analysis, 'multi-trait multi-method' matrices, external validity coefficients, etc. —for documenting individual differences. Rather, his preferred method is a somewhat impressionistic analysis based on a convergence of signs provided by eight different lines of evidence.

Chief among these signs are isolation by brain damage, such that one form of intelligence can be selectively impaired, leaving other forms relatively unimpaired; and exceptional cases, individuals who possess extraordinary levels of ability in one domain, against a background of normal or even impaired abilities in other domains (alternatively, a person may show extraordinarily low levels of ability in one domain, against a background of normal or exceptionally high levels of ability in others). So, for example, Gardner (1983) argues from neurological case studies that damage to the prefrontal lobes of the cerebral cortex can selectively impair personal and social intelligence, leaving other abilities intact. The classic case of Phineas Gage may serve as an example (Macmillan, 1986). On the other hand, Luria's (1972) case of Zazetsky, "the man with a shattered world", sustained damage in the occipital and parietal lobes which severely impaired most of his intellectual capacities, but left his personal and social abilities relatively intact. Gardner also notes that while both Down syndrome and Alzheimer's disease have severe cognitive consequences but little impact on the person's ability to get along with other people, Pick's disease spares at least some cognitive abilities while severely impairing the person's ability to interact with others. In related work, Taylor and Cadet (1989) have proposed that three different brain systems provide the neurological substrate of social intelligence: a balanced or integrated cortical subsystem which relies on long-term memory to make complex social judgments; a frontal-dominant sub-system which organises and generates social behaviours; and a limbic-dominant sub-system which rapidly produces emotional responses to events. However, it should be noted that, with the exception of emotion (for an authoritative summary, see LeDoux, 1996; see also Kihlstrom, Mulvaney, Tobias, and Tobis, 1998), research on the neurological underpinnings of social cognition and behaviour is highly impressionistic and speculative (for a review of neuropsychological approaches to social cognition and social intelligence, see Klein and Kihlstrom, 1998).

With respect to exceptional individuals, Gardner offers Sigmund Freud and Marcel Proust as "prodigies" in the domain of intrapersonal intelligence, and Mahatma Gandhi and Lyndon Johnson as their counterparts in the domain of interpersonal intelligence. Each of these individuals, Gardner claims, displayed high levels of personal and social intelligence against a background of more "normal" abilities in other domains. On the negative side, Gardner notes that infantile autism (Kanner's syndrome, Williams' syndrome, etc.) severely impairs the individual's ability to understand other people and navigate the social world.

In addition, Gardner postulates several other signs suggesting different types of intelligence. Among these are identifiable core operations, coupled with experimental tasks which permit analysis of these core operations and psychometric tests which reveal individual differences in ability to perform them. With respect to social intelligence, of course, the core operations are those which form the core of research on social cognition: person perception and impression formation, causal attribution, person memory, social categorisation, impression management, and the like. The social cognition literature offers numerous paradigms for studying these operations, of course, and sometimes these experimental procedures have been translated into techniques for the analysis of individual differences (e.g., Kihlstrom and Nasby, 1981; Nasby and Kihlstrom, 1985). For example, Kaess and Witryol (1955) studied memory for names and faces; Sechrest and Jackson (1961) examined individual differences in the ability to predict other people's behaviour in various kinds of situations; and Sternberg and his colleagues (Barnes and Sternberg, 1989; Sternberg and Smith, 1985) have assessed individual differences in the ability to decode non-verbal communications.

Whether the core operations involved in social cognition differ qualitatively from those involved non-social cognition is, however, an open question. While perceiving emotion in a face may appear to differ qualitatively from mentally rotating an image of the letter R, a working assumption in most social cognition research is that the underlying mental processes are the same as those deployed in non-social cognition. Thus, for example, Cantor and Mischel (1979)'s research on prototypes in person perception was intended as a fairly direct translation of Rosch's (1978) pioneering work on fuzzy-set approaches to non-social categories. And while it is quite plausible to suggest that the perception of faces, those most social of stimuli, follows special rules and is mediated by a special brain area (e.g., Farah, 1996), recent experimental and neuroimaging evidence indicates that face recognition is simply an instance of a broader expertise for identifying objects at subordinate levels of categorisation (Gauthier, 1998).

One potentially important difference between the social and non-social domains, of course, is that in social cognition the object (i.e., the person) represented in the observer's mind is intelligent and conscious. Thus, the person being perceived may try to control the impression formed by the perceiver through a variety of impression-management strategies (Goffman, 1959; Jones and Pittman, 1982). To complicate things further, the perceiver may well be aware of the possibility of strategic self-presentation, and thus adjust his or her perceptions accordingly, while the person being perceived may modulate his or her impression-management activities so as to minimise these corrections. Such interaction rituals (Goffman, 1967) are not likely to occur in non-social perception and cognition.

In addition to experimental and psychometric evidence, Gardner (1983) also assumes that qualitatively different forms of intelligence will show distinctive developmental histories. From an ontogenetic point of view, then, the hypothesis is that the acquisition and mastery of competencies in the social domain follows a different developmental trajectory, from infancy through adolescence and adulthood to old age, than other abilities. Similarly, from a phylogenetic point of view, the hypothesis would be that personal and interpersonal abilities trace different evolutionary pathways as well. Thus, Gardner (1983) cites Gallup's (1970, 1998; Gallup, Marino, and Eddy, 1997) finding that humans and chimpanzees, but not other primates (and not other mammals) pass the mirror-image test of self-recognition.

Finally, Gardner argues that each form of intelligence is encoded in a unique symbol system by which the ability in question can be manipulated and transmitted by a culture. For some of his proposed intelligences, the existence of the symbol system is fairly obvious: written language, mathematical symbols, and musical notation are clear examples. As evidence suggestive of special personal symbol systems, Gardner cites Geertz's (1975) ethnographic work in Java, Bali, and Morocco, which revealed considerable cultural diversity in the means by which people maintain a sense of self and the rules which govern their social relations — personal and social intelligence which is acquired through socialisation. Certainly, the English language contains a large vocabulary of words — 17,953 by one count (Allport and Odbert, 1937) — which can represent people's cognitive, emotional, and motivational states, behavioural dispositions, and other psycho-social characteristics. And within Western culture, structures like the classic four-fold classification of temperament (melancholic, phlegmatic, choleric, and sanguine; Kant, 1798/1978) and the Big Five personality dimensions (neuroticism, extraversion, agreeableness, conscientiousness, and openness to experience; John, 1990) are commonly employed to capture and communicate the gist of another person's personality.

Prototype of Social Intelligence

Although social intelligence has proved difficult for psychometricians to operationalise, it does appear to play a major role in people's naive, intuitive concepts of intelligence. Following up on earlier work by Rosch (1978), Cantor (Cantor and Mischel, 1979; Cantor, Smith, French, and Mezzich, 1980), and Neisser (1979), Sternberg and his colleagues asked subjects to list the behaviours which they considered characteristic of intelligence, academic intelligence, everyday intelligence, and unintelligence; two additional groups of subjects rated each of 250 behaviours from the first list in terms of how "characteristic" each was of the ideal person possessing each of the three forms of intelligence (Sternberg, Conway, Ketron, and Bernstein, 1981). Factor analysis of ratings provided by lay people yielded a factor of "social competence" in each context.

Prototypical behaviours reflecting social competence were:

Accepts others for what they are;

Admits mistakes;

Displays interest in the world at large;

Is on time for appointments;

Has social conscience;

Thinks before speaking and doing;

Displays curiosity;

Does not make snap judgements;

Makes fair judgements;

Assesses well the relevance of information to a problem at hand;

Is sensitive to other people's needs and desires;

Is frank and honest with self and others; and

Displays interest in the immediate environment.

Interestingly, a separate dimension of social competence did not consistently emerge in ratings made by a group of experts on intelligence. Rather, the experts' dimensions focussed on verbal intelligence and problem-solving ability, with social competence expressly emerging only in the ratings of the ideal "practically intelligent" person. Perhaps these experts shared Wechsler's (1939) dismissive view of social intelligence.

A similar study was performed by Kosmitzki and John (1993). Based largely on prior research by Orlik (1978), these investigators assembled a list of 18 features which make up people's implicit concept of social intelligence. When subjects were asked to rate how necessary each feature was to their own personal understanding of social intelligence, the following dimensions emerged as most central to the prototype:

Understands people's thoughts, feelings, and intentions well;

Is good at dealing with people;

Has extensive knowledge of rules and norms in human relations;

Is good at taking the perspective of other people;

Adapts well in social situations;

Is warm and caring; and

Is open to new experiences, ideas, and values.

In another part of the study, subjects were asked to rate someone they liked on each of these attributes. After statistically controlling for differential likability of the traits, a factor analysis yielded a clear dimension of social intelligence, defined by the attributes listed above. The remaining two factors were named social influence and social memory.

A recent psychometric study of social intelligence used a methodology similar to that of Sternberg, et al. (1981) and Kosmitzki and John (1993). Schneider, Ackerman, and Kanfer (1996) asked subjects to generate descriptions of socially competent behaviour. These descriptors were then collated and reduced to form a Social Competence Questionnaire, in which subjects are asked to rate the extent to which each item described their typical social behaviour. A factor analysis revealed seven dimensions of social competence: extraversion, warmth, social influence, social insight, social openness, social appropriateness, and social maladjustment. Composite scores on these dimensions were essentially uncorrelated with measures of quantitative and verbal/reasoning ability. On the basis of these findings, Schneider, et al. concluded that "it is time to lay to rest any residual notions that social competence is a monolithic entity, or that it is just general intelligence applied to social situations". As with Marlowe's (1986) study, however, the reliance on self-report measures of social intelligence compromises this conclusion, which remains to be confirmed using objective performance measures of the various dimensions in the social domain.

Sternberg, et al. (1981) has noted that in contrast to explicit theories of intelligence, which attempt to explain what intelligence is, implicit theories attempt to capture people's views of what the word intelligence means. Social intelligence played little role in Sternberg's early componential view of human intelligence (Sternberg, 1977, 1980; Sternberg, 1984), which was intended to focus on reasoning and problem-solving skills as represented by traditional intelligence tests. However, social intelligence is explicitly represented in Sternberg's more recent triarchic view of intelligence (Sternberg, 1984, 1985, 1988). According to the triarchic theory, intelligence is composed of analytical, creative, and practical abilities. Practical intelligence is defined in terms of problem-solving in everyday contexts, and explicitly includes social intelligence (Sternberg and Wagner, 1986). According to Sternberg, each type of intelligence reflects the operation of three different kinds of component processes: performance components, which solve problems in various domains; executive meta components, which plan and evaluate problem-solving; and knowledge-acquisition components, by which the first two components are learned. To complicate things further, Sternberg (1985, 1988) argues that the measurement of all forms of intelligence is sensitive to the context in which it is assessed. This may be especially the case for practical and social intelligence: for example, the correct answer to a question of social judgment may well be different if it is posed in a corporate (Wagner and Sternberg, 1985) or military (Legree, 1995) context.

For Sternberg, these abilities, and thus their underlying components, may well be somewhat independent of each other. There is no implication, for example, that a person who is strong on analytical intelligence will also be strong in creative and practical intelligence. In any event, the relation among various intellectual abilities is an empirical question. Answering this question, of course, requires that we have adequate instruments for assessing social intelligence — tests which adequately sample the domain in question, in addition to being reliable and valid. At present, these instruments do not appear to exist. However, future investigators who wish to make the attempt might be well advised to begin with the intuitive concept of social intelligence held in the mind of the layperson. After all, social intelligence is a social construct, not just an academic one.

Personality as Social Intelligence

In contrast to the psychometric approaches reviewed above, the social intelligence view of personality (Cantor and Kihlstrom, 1987, 1989; Cantor and Fleeson, 1994; Cantor and Harlow, 1994; Kihlstrom and Cantor, 1989; Cantor and Kihlstrom, 1982; Cantor and Zirkel, 1990; Snyder and Cantor, 1998) does not conceptualise social intelligence as a trait, or group of traits, on which individuals can be compared and ranked on a dimension from low to high. Rather, the social-intelligence view of personality begins with the assumption that social behaviour is intelligent—that it is mediated by cognitive processes of perception, memory, reasoning, and problem-solving, rather than being mediated by innate reflexes, conditioned responses, evolved genetic programmes, and the like. Accordingly, the social intelligence view construes individual differences in social behaviour— the public manifestations of personality — to be the product of individual differences in the knowledge which individuals bring to bear on their social interactions. Differences in social knowledge cause differences in social behaviour, but it does not make sense to construct measures of social IQ. The important variable is not how much social intelligence the person has, but rather what social intelligence he or she possesses.

Social Intelligence in Life Tasks

Although the social intelligence view of personality diverges from the psychometric approach to social intelligence on the matter of assessment, it agrees with some contemporary psychometric views that intelligence is context-specific. Thus, in Sternberg's (1985, 1988) triarchic theory, social intelligence is part of a larger repertoire of knowledge by which the person attempts to solve the practical problems encountered in the physical and social world. According to Cantor and Kihlstrom (1987), social intelligence is specifically geared to solving the problems of social life, and in particular managing the life tasks, current concerns (Klinger 1977) or personal projects (Little, 1989) which the person selects for him—or herself, or which other people impose on him or her from outside. Put another way, one's social intelligence cannot be evaluated in the abstract, but only with respect to the domains and contexts in which it is exhibited and the life tasks it is designed to serve. And even in this case, "adequacy" cannot be judged from the viewpoint of the external observer, but rather from the point of view of the subject whose life tasks are in play.

Life tasks provide an integrative unit of analysis for the analysis of the interaction between the person and the situation. They may be explicit or implicit, abstract or circumscribed, universal or unique, enduring or stage-specific, rare or commonplace, ill-defined or well-defined problems. Whatever their features, they give meaning to the individual's life, and serve to organise his or her daily activities. They are defined from the subjective point of view of the individual: they are the tasks which the person perceives him—or herself as "working on and devoting energy to solving during a specified period in life (Cantor and Kihlstrom, 1987). First and foremost, life tasks are articulated by the individual as self-relevant, time-consuming, and meaningful. They provide a kind of organising scheme for the individual's activities, and they are embedded in the individual's on-going daily life. And they are responsive to the demands, structure, and constraints of the social environment in which the person lives. Life tasks are imposed on people, and the ways in which they are approached may be constrained by socio-cultural factors. However, unlike the stage-structured views of Erikson (1950) and his popularisers (e.g., Levinson, 1978; Sheehy, 1976), the social-intelligence view of personality does not propose that everyone at a particular age is engaged in the same sorts of life tasks. Instead, periods of transition, where the person is entering into new institutions, are precisely those times where individual differences in life tasks become most apparent.

For example, Cantor and her associates have chosen the transition from high school to college as a particularly informative period to investigate life tasks (Cantor, Acker, and Cook-Flanagan, 1992; Cantor and Fleeson, 1991, 1994; Cantor and Harlow, 1994; Cantor and Langston, 1989; Cantor and Malley, 1991; Cantor, Norem, Langston, Zirkel, Fleeson, and

Cook-Flanagan, 1991; Cantor, Norem, Niedenthal, Langston, and Brower, 1987; Zirkel and Cantor, 1990). Freshman year is more than just convenient for academic researchers to study: The transition from high school to college and adulthood is a critical developmental milestone, where many individuals leave home for the first time to establish various independent habits and life styles. And although the decision to attend college may have been made for them (or may not have been a decision at all, but just a fact of life), students still have a great deal of leeway to decide for themselves that they are going to do with the opportunity—what life tasks will occupy them for the next four years. Accordingly, when college students are asked to list their life tasks, they list social life tasks (e.g., making friends or being on my own) as often as they list academic ones (e.g., getting good grades or carving a future direction). And while the majority of students' life tasks could be slotted into a relatively small number of common categories, their individual construal of these tasks were quite unique, and led to equally unique strategies for action.

The intelligent nature of life-task pursuit is clearly illustrated by the strategies deployed in its service. People often begin to comprehend the problem at hand by simulating a set of plausible outcomes, relating them to previous experiences stored in autobiographical memory. They also formulate specific plans for action, and monitor their progress toward the goal, taking special note of environmental factors which stand in the way, and determining whether the actual outcome meets their original expectations. Much of the cognitive activity in life-task problem solving involves forming causal attributions about outcomes, and in surveying autobiographical memory for hints about how things might have gone differently. Particularly compelling evidence of the intelligent nature of life task pursuit comes when, inevitably, plans go awry or some unforeseen event frustrates progress. Then, the person will map out a new path toward the goal, or even choose a new goal compatible with a super ordinate life task. Intelligence frees us from reflex, tropism, and instinct, in social life as in non-social domains.

Development of Social Intelligence

Although the psychometric and personality views of social intelligence are opposed on many important points, such as the matter of comparative assessment of individuals, they come together nicely in recent work on the development of social intelligence (for reviews, see Greenspan, 1979; Greenspan, 1997). Of course, social intelligence has always played a role in the concept of mental retardation. This psychiatric diagnosis requires not only evidence of subnormal intellectual functioning (i.e., IQ < 70) but also demonstrated evidence of impairments in "communication, self-care, home living, social and interpersonal skills, use of community resources, self-direction, functional academic skills, work, leisure, health, and safety" (American Psychiatric Association, 1994,). In other words, the diagnosis of mental retardation involves deficits in social as well as academic intelligence. Furthermore, the wording of the diagnostic criteria implies that social and academic intelligence are not highly correlated—it requires positive evidence of both forms of impairment, meaning that the presence of one cannot be inferred from the presence of the other.

While the conventional diagnostic criterion for mental retardation places primary emphasis on IQ and intellectual functioning Greenspan (1979) has argued that it should emphasise social and practical intelligence instead. To this end, Greenspan proposed a hierarchical model of social intelligence. In this model, social intelligence consists of three components: social sensitivity, reflected in role-taking and social inference; social insight, including social comprehension, psychological insight, and moral judgement; and social communication subsuming referential communication and social problem solving. Social intelligence, in turn, is only one component of adaptive intelligence (the others being conceptual intelligence and practical intelligence), which in turn joins physical competence and socio-emotional adaptation (temperament and character) as the major dimensions of personal competence broadly construed. Greenspan did not propose specific tests for any of these components of social intelligence, but implied that they could be derived from experimental procedures used to study social cognition in general.

All this is well and good, but while the criterion for impaired intellectual functioning is clearly operationalised by an IQ threshold, there is as yet no standard by which impaired social functioning — impaired social intelligence can be determined. The Vineland Social Maturity Scale (Doll, 1947) was an important step in this direction: this instrument, which yields aggregate scores of social age (analogous to mental age) and social quotient (by analogy to the intelligence quotient, calculated as social age divided by chronological age). However, it is a telling point that this instrument for evaluating social intelligence and other aspects of adaptive behaviour was introduced almost a half century after the first IQ scale was introduced by Binet and Simon. The Vineland, which has been recently revised (Sparrow, Balla, and Cicchetti, 1984), but its adequacy as a measure of social intelligence is compromised by the fact that linguistic functions, motor skills, occupational skills, and self-care and self-direction are assessed as well as social relations. As an alternative, Taylor (1990) has proposed a semi structured Social Intelligence Interview covering such domains as social memory, moral development, recognition of and response to social cues, and social judgment. However, Taylor concedes that such an interview, being ideographically constructed to take account of the individual's particular social environment, cannot easily yield numerical scores by which individuals can be compared and ranked. More important than ranking individuals, from Taylor's point of view, is identify areas of high and low functioning within various environments experienced by the individual, and to determine the goodness of fit between the individual and the environments in which he or she lives. This latter goal, of course, is a primary thrust of the social intelligence view of personality espoused by Cantor and Kihlstrom (1987).

A further step away from the psychometric emphasis on ranking toward the social-cognitive emphasis on general processes is illustrated by recent trends in research on autism. Specifically, it has been proposed by Leslie (1987) and Baron-Cohen (1995), among others, that autistic children and adults lack a "theory of mind" (Premack and Woodruff, 1978; see also Flavell, Green, and Flavell, 1995; Gopnik and Meltzoff, 1997;

Wellman, 1990) by which they can attribute mental states to other people and reflect on their own mental life (for a summary review, see Klein and Kihlstrom, 1998). For example, Baron-Cohen, Leslie, and Frith (1985) suggested that the core deficit in autism is that the affected children are unable to appreciate that other people's beliefs, attitudes, and experiences might differ from their own. This hypothesis brought the problem of assessing social intelligence in disabled populations (including mental retardation and learning disability as well as autism; see Greenspan and Love, 1997) directly in contact with a literature on the development of social cognition in normal children which had been emerging since the 1970s (Flavell, 1974; Flavell and Ross, 1981; Shantz, 1975). In this way, scientific understanding of social cognition in general began to influence research and theory on individual differences in social cognition.

Still, the problem remains. Is the core deficit in autism one of social intelligence, as Baron-Cohen (1995) claims? In this respect, it is interesting to note, along with Gardner (1983), that autistic individuals can show an impaired ability to understand others' mental states, but spared abilities to deal cognitively with non-social objects and events, as well as to comprehend social situations where they are not required to understand another persons knowledge, belief, feelings, and desires. On the other hand, Bruner and Feldman (1993) have proposed that these deficits in social cognition are secondary to deficits in general cognitive functioning. Thus, although research on normal and abnormal development is more closely in contact with general social-cognitive theory than before, the fundamental questions endure: Is social cognition a separate faculty from non-social cognition? Is social intelligence anything different from general intelligence applied to the social domain?

As psychologists are fond of saying, further research is needed to answer these questions. However, we can hope that future research on social intelligence will have a different character than it has had in the past. One of the most salient, and distressing, features of the history of intelligence is how little contact there has been between the instruments by which we assess individual differences in intellectual ability and our understanding of the processes which supply the cognitive substrate of intellectual ability (Sternberg, 1977). The IQ test, once touted as "psychology's most telling accomplishment to date" (Herrnstein, 1974), is almost entirely a theoretical, having been pragmatically constructed to model the sorts of things which children do in school. So too with social intelligence, which all too often has been conceptualised informally, and assessed by means of a jury-rigged assortment of tests (Walker and Foley, 1973). Perhaps new theoretical approaches, such as the social-intelligence view of personality and the "theory of mind" view of development, will change this situation, so that future reviews of this sort will be able to describe assessments of social intelligence which are grounded in an understanding of the general social-cognitive processes out of which individual differences in social behaviour emerge.

SOCIAL INTELLIGENCE AND ALLIED ASPECTS

Gautama, P. N. (1974) reported that, in general, the patterns of social interaction found in the sample were also prevalent in rural and urban boys' and girls' schools barring certain minor variations.

Vora, J.I. (1980) found that the student-teachers coming from the urban areas were more socially mature than the student teachers from the rural areas.

Nayal, Shanti (1990) observed regarding social responsibility, rural and urban students were similar.

Pandey (1979) found that among higher secondary stage, the rural group was to be better in emotional, health and school adjustment whereas the urban group was better in aesthetic adjustment. Significant relationship exists between adjustment, aspiration and achievement.

Sharma, G.R. (1978) reported that the non-professional college students had more problems than the professional college students in the area of social adjustment. The medical students and the science students had greater problems in social, emotional and educational areas than the commerce students.

Saovaluk Thongngamkhom (1983) found that the students having good personal social-adjustment were more socially matured than those having poor personal-social adjustment.

Patel, M.G.(1981) reported that as the age increased, the students became more sociable.

Saxena, G. (1992) reported that the girls led a more protected life with restricted movements; the girls and the boys differed in responses to items on the places visited, living and eating arrangements, marital status, social and economic background and courses offered.

Rao, N. (1978) found a significant positive relationship between social maturity and intelligence.

Tara, P. (1980) observed that boys showed a significantly superior scores in comparison to girls on various measures of self-concept such as behaviour, intellectual and school status and physical appearance and attributes with the sole exception of popularity where the two groups were similar.

Vora, J.I. (1980) reported that the male student teachers were superior to the female student teachers in social maturity.

Magotra, H.P. (1982) found that girls scored higher in the intelligence test than boys.

Nayal, Shanti (1990) reported that regarding social responsibility, the female students were superior to the male students.

Pathak R.D. (1971) noticed that the popular students in a socio-metric scale are significantly superior in home adjustment, social adjustment, emotional adjustment, school adjustment and health adjustment.

Tulpule (1977) reported that 80 per cent are emotionally maladjusted, 30 per cent poorly socially adjusted, 25 per cent poorly adjusted at home, 30 per cent health-wise maladjusted and 58 per cent generally maladjusted.

Prakash, V. (1986) reported that boys having a university position were more intelligent than those having university participation. Similarly boys having an inter-university position were more intelligent than those having university participation. Boys having a university position were more intelligent than the inter-university position group. Boys with high socio-economic status were more intelligent than those with middle and low socio-economic status.

Sultana, M. (1983) found that there was a significant difference in intelligence between normal and clinical subjects, normal were more intelligent. Deviant children were less socially competent in comparison with the normal group.

Arunima (1989) reported that aggressive children scored lower on intelligence than non-aggressive children.

Asthna, Anju (1989) found that intelligence academic achievement, and adult-dependence was significantly associated with the social maturity of children, although adult-dependence had a negative association.

Agnihotri, C.S. (1991) observed that social maturity and educational adjustment were only the social ingredients. Psychological characteristics also influenced the social maturity and educational adjustment of the children.

Vishistha (1981) noticed that poor adjustment along with authoritarianism, and conservatism creates alienation among students. These traits also contribute to growth and development of feelings of powerlessness, normalness and social isolation. Poor adjustment in social life is reported to be a significant condition for the development of feeling of life alienation.

Pathak R.D. (1971) reported that the populars were significantly superior to all the other three groups in social adjustment and emotional adjustment.

Dhillon, G.K. (1979) observed that in all aspects of school adjustment, adjustment with schoolmates, administration, and teachers and with self, the participants scored significantly higher than non-participants. No significant sex differences were obtained on the dimension of school adjustment.

Gupta A.K. (1981) found that adolescents from joint families tended to exhibit significantly better educational, social and emotional adjustment.

Tulpule (1977) reported that in the area of social adjustment, thirty per cent showed poor adjustment and submissive, retiring, tendency. Six per cent indicated aggressiveness in social contacts. In the area of emotional adjustment about eighty per cent of the girls were found to be emotionally maladjusted, seventeen per cent showed average adjustment and only three per cent were found to be well adjusted.

These studies are not directly related to the social intelligence of prospective teachers as there are no such studies on record. Hence, the present study on the social intelligence of prospective teachers.

3

RESEARCH DESIGN

Research is a systematic enquiry seeking facts through objective and verifiable methods in order to discover the relationship among them and to deduce from them the broad principles or laws. Therefore, the very success of a research work depends upon collecting the necessary information. Several methods of collecting information are developed to assist the research. Every survey expert has his own ideas of selecting the best method of collecting information. But, it cannot be uniform to all. Selection of the method depends on the type of information to be gathered and the sources of information to be consulted. For thc present study, normative survey method is chosen.

Survey means viewing and interpreting things rigorously and comprehensively. Now-a-days, survey method is a popular way of collecting data for analysing the results statistically and systematically. This method is suitable to this study as this one is a status study.

OPERATIONAL DEFINITIONS OF KEY TERMS

The operational definitions of the important key terms used in the present study are explained hereunder:

Study

Study refers to a systematic investigation which is objective and research oriented.

Intelligence

The capacity to acquire and apply knowledge and skill is intelligence.

Social Intelligence

Social intelligence is the ability of an individual to react to social situations of daily life.

Student Teacher

The would be teachers who are studying B.Ed. Course.

Rural Student Teacher

Student who is studying B.Ed. course in rural areas, i.e., villages.

Urban Student Teacher

Student who is studying B.Ed. course in urban areas i.e., towns and cities.

Graduate Student Teacher

Student teacher who completed B.Sc., B.A. and B.Com., and pursuing B.Ed. course.

Postgraduate Student Teacher

Student teacher who completed M.Sc., M.A., M.Com. and studying B.Ed. course.

Gender

Gender refers to male and female student teachers.

Locality

Locality refers to rural and urban areas.

Methodology

Methodology refers to the method of study under which the student has been admitted into the B.Ed. course. For the present study Arts and Science teaching methodologies were considered.

- Arts methodology, wherein the student teacher studies social studies as the elective subject.
- Science methodology, wherein the student studies biological science or mathematics (or) physical science as the elective subject.

VARIABLES OF THE STUDY

Variables are the conditions or characteristics that the experimenter manipulates, controls or observes. There are mainly three types of variables, namely, independent, dependent and intervening. The independent variables are those variables which do not change on manipulation by the experimenter. The dependent variables are those variables which change on manipulation done by the experimenter. The intervening variables are those variables which are dependent both on dependent and independent variables.

For the present study, the following independent variables are chosen:

Gender

Male and Female Student Teachers.

Locality

Rural and Urban Student Teachers.

Methodology

Arts and Science Teaching Methodology Student Teachers

Educational Qualifications

Graduate and Postgraduate Student Teachers.

HYPOTHESES OF THE STUDY

Hypothesis is the most important step in the research process. It is a tentative supposition or provisional guess which seems to explain the situation under observation. The following hypotheses are formulated based on the variables and objectives of the study. These were stated in "null hypothesis" form. The null hypothesis states that there is no significant difference or relationship between two or more parameters. It concerns to a judgement at whether apparent differences or relationships are true or whether they merely result from sampling.

The hypotheses of the present study are:

1. The student teachers are not holding high social intelligence;
2. There is no significant difference in the social intelligence of male and female student teachers;
3. There is no significant difference in the social intelligence of rural and urban student teachers;
4. There is no significant difference in the social intelligence of student teachers of Arts and Science teaching methodology;
5. There is no significant difference in the social intelligence of graduate and post graduate student teachers.

SAMPLE OF THE STUDY

A sample is a smaller representation of the larger whole. A sample contains primarily sampling units and a slice of the population representing the universe. A sample must possess the following essential characteristics to provide accurate results. They are representativeness, adequacy, homogeneity, lack of bias, smallness in size, accuracy and completeness.

The population for the study refers to all the student teachers who undergo one year B.Ed. course in the Colleges of Education of Guntur district.

Sampling is the easiest method for social investigation. The purpose of sampling is to draw inferences concerning the universe. There are three elements in the process of sampling. They are: Selection of sample; collection of information; and drawing of inferences. According to Cornell, sampling is the process by which a relatively small number of individuals are selected or analysed in order to find out something about the entire population or the universe from which it is selected.

In any research, various methods are utilised for selection of samples. After a detailed study of all the methods, the stratified random sampling method was selected for the present study. Stratified random sampling is applied as this method of selection assures each individual element in the universe of equal chance of being chosen. This is suitable for the present study of the universe considered for the study is homogenous. In order to reduce the sampling error, a sample of 307 was chosen.

In this study, the strata divided are represented in the following table:

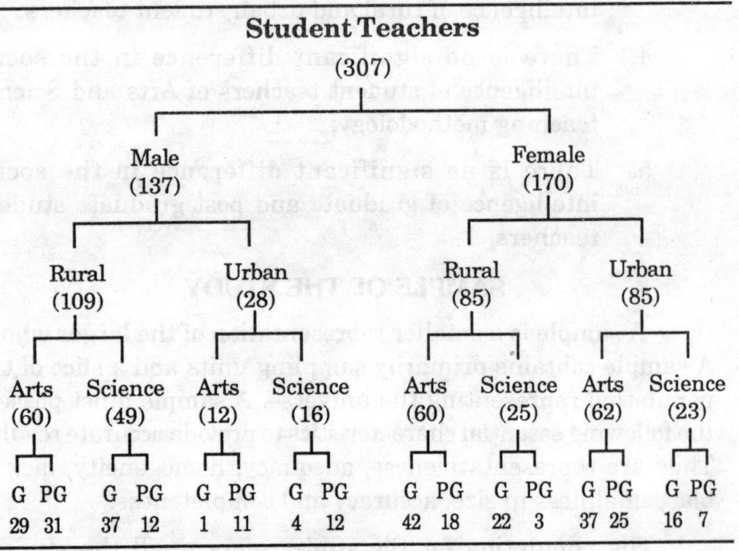

G - Graduate; PG - Postgraduate

TOOL OF THE STUDY

A research tool plays a major role in any worthwhile research, as it is the sole factor in determining sound data and in arriving at perfect conclusions about the problem or study in hand, which ultimately helps in providing suitable remedial measures to the problem concerned. The selection and use of tool can be done in two ways. The first one is to construct a tool independently by the researcher and the second one is to select a standardised tool that is already available in the field of study.

The tool used in the present study is "Social Intelligence Scale" standardised by N.K. Chadha and Usha Ganesan.

The scale measures the following of social intelligence.

- *Patience*- Calm endurance under stressful situations.
- *Cooperativeness*: Ability to interact with others in a pleasant way to be able to view matters from all angles.
- *Confidence Level*: Firm trust in oneself and ones chances.
- *Sensitivity*: To be acutely aware of and responsive to human behaviour.
- *Recognition of Social Environment*: Ability to perceive the nature and atmosphere of the existing situation.
- *Tactfulness*: Delicate perception of the right thing to say or do.
- *Sense of Humour*: Capacity to feel and cause amusement; to be able to see the lighter side of life.
- *Memory:* Ability to remember all relevant issues; names and faces of people.

Administration of the Tool

The tool was administered personally by the researcher on the student teachers and the sample was asked to respond to the statements. Before giving the tool to the participants, the researcher explained the purpose of the present investigation. Directions given on the cover sheet were read out to the participants and specific instructions were given.

4

ANALYSIS OF DATA

Analysis of the data is the most skilled task of all stages of research. It depends on the judgment and skill of the researcher. It should be done by the researcher and should not be entrusted to another person. Analysis of data means studying the tabulated material in order to determine inherent facts or meanings. It involves breaking down complex factors into simple one and putting the parts in new arrangements for the purpose of interpretation.

The method of analysis chosen for a particular study depends upon the nature of objectives, hypotheses to be tested, the purpose and use of the study. Statistical methods are the mathematical techniques used to facilitate the interpretation of numerical data secured from groups of individuals or group of observations or a single individual. A basic knowledge about statistics becomes inevitable for research workers, for systematic analysis and accurate and precise interpretation of data.

For the present study, several statistical techniques were used to perform the analysis. After collecting the data from three hundred and seven perspective teachers through a standardised tool, the analysis was performed keeping in view objectives framed, hypotheses formulated, type of data collected, type of tool used, etc. For this purpose, mean, standard deviation, normal probability, critical ratio, etc., were employed.

Social Intelligence and Student Teachers

The student teachers are not holding high social intelligence.

To test the validity of this hypothesis, the total scores of the whole sample were used to calculate the mean and S.D. The results are as follows:

Table 4.1

Social Intelligence of Student Teachers

Sample	*Sample Size*	*Mean*	*Standard Deviation*
Whole	307	108.92	5.84

From the mean value of Table 4.1, it is evident that there was a high social intelligence in student teachers.

The hypothesis that "the student teachers are not holding high social intelligence" can be rejected as the prospective teachers are possessing a high social intelligence.

Social Intelligence and Gender

There is no significant difference in the social intelligence of male and female student teachers.

To test the validity of Hypothesis 2, the following calculations were carried out:

Table 4.2

Comparison of Social Intelligence of Male and Female Student Teachers

Variable	*Sample Size*	*Mean*	*S.D.*	*Difference of Means*	*S.E.D.*	*Critical Ratio*
Male	137	109.35	6.31	0.78	0.67	1.164*
Female	170	108.57	5.41			

* Not Significant at 0.05 Level.

From the value of Table 4.2, it is evident that both male and female student teachers were with high social intelligence without any significant difference between them.

The hypothesis that "there is no significant difference in the social intelligence of male and female student teachers" can be accepted as there is no significant difference in the level of social intelligence of male and female student teachers.

Social Intelligence and Locality

There is no significant difference in the social intelligence of rural and urban student teachers.

To test the validity of the Hypothesis 3, the following calculations were made:

Table 4.3

Comparison of Social Intelligence of Rural and Urban Student Teachers

Variable	*Sample Size*	*Mean*	*S.D.*	*Difference of Means*	*S.E.D.*	*Critical Ratio*
Rural	194	109.35	5.84	1.17	0.68	1.72*
Urban	113	108.17	5.84			

* Not significant at 0.05 level.

From the value of Table 4.3, it is clear that both rural and urban student teachers were with high social intelligence without any significant difference between them.

The hypothesis that "there is no significant difference in the social intelligence of rural and urban student teachers" can be accepted as there is no significant difference in the level of social intelligence of rural and urban student teachers.

Social Intelligence and Teaching Methodology

There is no significant difference in the social intelligence of arts and science methodology student teachers.

To test the validity of Hypothesis 4, the following calculations were carried out:

Table 4.4

Comparison of Social Intelligence of
Arts and Science Methodology Student Teachers

Variable	*Sample Size*	*Mean*	*S.D.*	*Difference of Means*	*S.E.D.*	*Critical Ratio*
Arts Teachers	194	108.48	5.83	1.17	0.69	1.695*
Science Teachers	113	109.66	5.86			

* Not Significant at 0.05 Level.

From the value of Table 4.4, it is clear that arts and science methodology student teachers had high social intelligence with no significant difference between them.

The hypothesis that "there is no significant difference in the social intelligence of arts and science methodology student teachers" can be accepted as there is no significant difference in the level of social intelligence of arts and science methodology student teachers.

Social Intelligence and Qualification

There is no significant difference in the social intelligence of graduate and postgraduate student teachers.

To test the validity of Hypothesis 5, the following calculations were calculated:

Table 4.5

Comparison of Social Intelligence of
Graduate and Postgraduate Student Teachers

Variable	*Sample Size*	*Mean*	*S.D.*	*Difference of Means*	*S.E.D.*	*Critical Ratio*
Graduates	188	108.75	5.84	0.44	0.68	0.64*
Post-graduates	119	109.19	5.85			

* Not Significant at 0.05 level.

From the value of table 4.5, it is evident that graduate and postgraduate student teachers were with high social intelligence. There was no significant difference between them in the level of social intelligence possessed.

The hypothesis that "there is no significant difference in the social intelligence of graduate and postgraduate student teachers" can be accepted as their is no significant difference in the level of social intelligence of graduate and postgraduate student teachers.

5

SUMMARY, CONCLUSIONS AND DISCUSSION

Basically, intelligence is conceived as a specific word. As Dookrell (1970) put it, intelligence might be taken to mean ability. Earlier definitions have termed it "the ability to judge all, to comprehend well, to reason well" (Binet); "the capacity to form concepts and grasp their significance"; "all-around thinking capacity or mental efficiency" (Vernon); "innate, general cognitive ability" (Binet); "grasping the essentials in a situation and responding appropriately to them" (Helm); "adaptation to the physical and social environment" (Piaget); "the aggregate or global capacity of the individual to act purposefully, to deal rationally and to deal effectively with the environment" (Weschler).

An operational definition proposed is that intelligence is what intelligence tests measure. Vernon (1960) and Guilford (1967) discussed the biological, experimental and psychological, developmental and operational approaches to the study of intelligence. Many argue that intelligence is not the same as other psychological terms like "learning", "thinking", "problem solving", "attainment", or "achievement" (e.g., Turner, 1977). Some feel these terms are not qualitatively different and to great extent overlap (e.g., Humphreys, 1971; Mc Farland, 1971).

E.L. Thorndike has divided intelligent activity into three types:

1. Social intelligence, or ability to understand and deal with persons;
2. Concrete intelligence, or ability to understand and deal with things as in skilled trades and scientific appliances; and
3. Abstract intelligence, or ability to understand and deal with verbal and mathematical symbols.

Thorndike classified intelligence as concrete intelligence, abstract intelligence and social intelligence.

Social intelligence means ability of an individual to react to social situations of daily life. Social intelligence would not include the feelings or emotions aroused in us by other people, but merely our ability to understand others and to react in such a way towards them that the ends desired should be attained. High social intelligence is possessed by those who are able to handle people well. Adequate adjustment in social situation is the index of social intelligence. The human capacity to understand what is happening in the world and responding to that understanding in a personally and socially effective manner.

Social intelligence is the ability to get along well with others. Sometimes it is referred to simplistically as "people skills". Social intelligence includes an awareness of situations and the social dynamics that govern them and knowledge of interaction styles and strategies that can help a person achieve his or her objectives in dealing with others. It also involves a certain amount of self-insight and a consciousness of one's own perceptions and reaction patterns.

Social intelligence is not a part of personality. Social intelligence is one of a clusters of intelligences, according to the Theory of Multiple Intelligences advanced by Howard Gardner. Social intelligence can be measured measuring social intelligence involves identifying key interaction skills and then assessing them behaviourally. All human interaction takes place with some context or other and effectiveness involves mastering the contexts within which one is called upon to interact. Social intelligence can be learned or developed.

The problem of understanding the behaviour of people in "face-to face contacts", of "empathy", of "person perception", and of "social sensitivity", and "problems of influencing or managing the behaviour of others" have been recognised for a long time, but little systematic work has been done on basic understanding of those phenomena. E.L. Thorndike (1920) had pointed out that there is an aspect of personality that can be called "social intelligence", distinct from "concrete" and "abstract" intelligences. Guilford (1958) suggested that social intelligence could be accounted for as a fourth category of information. It carries the implication that there are 30 abilities involved in social intelligence as specified by structure of intellect.

Social intelligence is a construct that not only appeals to laymen as a relevant individual difference but also has shown promising practical applications. Nevertheless, the use of social intelligence in research and applied settings has been limited by definitional problems, difficulties in empirically differentiating social intelligence from related constructs, and the complexity of most existing measures of social intelligence.

The objectives of the study were:

1. To find out the social intelligence of student teachers;
2. To compare the social intelligence of male and female student teachers;
3. To compare the social intelligence of rural and urban student teachers;
4. To compare the social intelligence of arts and science student teachers;
5. To compare the social intelligence of graduate and postgraduate student teachers.

The normative survey method was used in the present study. This method investigates into the conditions and relationships that exist at present in the context of social intelligence of student teachers.

Variable is a condition or characteristic which the experimenter manipulates, controls or observes for the present study the variables chosen were:

1. Gender (male and female student teachers);
2. Locality (rural and urban student teachers);
3. Teaching Methodology (arts and science student teachers); and
4. Educational Qualification (graduate and postgraduate student teachers).

Hypotheses are guesses or tentative generalisations which provide basis to the whole study to be tested by facts. For the present study the hypotheses framed were:

1. The student teachers are not holding high social intelligence;
2. There is no significant difference in the social intelligence of male and female student teachers;
3. There is no significant difference in the social intelligence of rural and urban student teachers;
4. There is no significant difference in the social intelligence of arts and science methodology student teachers;
5. There is no significant difference in the social intelligence of graduate and postgraduate student teachers.

A sample is a small group which represents all the traits and characteristics of the population. The student teachers studying in Colleges of Education of Guntur district were selected as population. The stratified random sampling technique was used in selecting the sample. The sample was 307 (three hundred and seven) student teachers.

A research tool is a tool used for the purpose of data collection. The tool used in the present study was Social Intelligence Scale, standardised by N.K. Chadha and Usha Ganesan.

For the analysis of data, suitable statistical techniques like mean, standard deviation and critical ratio were used.

CONCLUSIONS AND DISCUSSION

From the analysis of the data, the following conclusions are drawn and these are followed by necessary discussion.

The student teachers possessed high level of social intelligence.

They are matured in age and also they have completed their graduation. They are in the middle of the B.Ed. course. So, they have developed social intelligence through learning aspects such as educational sociology, psychology, personality development, etc. They can mingle with all the people. They can understand others and adjust to the situation. Hence, they hold adequate social intelligence and this can be maintained further.

The male and female student teachers possessed high social intelligence without any significant difference between them.

In the present days, both female and male student teachers comfortably involve in the society. There are co-educational institutions and girls are studying in such institutions. Both of them are studying the same courses as such there is no difference between them in their social intelligence. This should be continued so as to make their students do well in the area of social intelligence.

The rural and urban student teachers possessed high social intelligence with no significant difference between them.

The rural and urban student teachers are having some adjustment with society. This is because they were participating together in social activities. This is continued and appropriate social interaction with students and other related personalities need to be maintained for furthering good behaviour of the students.

The student teachers of arts and science methodologies hold high social intelligence without any significant difference between them.

Social life is common for both arts and science student teachers. Their interaction with the members of the society is almost same. Hence there may no difference in the social intelligence of arts and science student teachers. Under this situation, the prospective teachers should help the students of their future classes do well in all spheres.

The graduate and postgraduate student teachers possessed high social intelligence with no significance between them.

As the qualification does not show any influence on the level of social intelligence, the prospective teachers should engage fully in their academic activities to enhance their abilities to because effective teachers in future. With these academic qualifications and high social intelligence, the student teachers will be of great use to the teaching community.

SUGGESTIONS FOR FURTHER RESEARCH

The present study, A Study of Social Intelligence of Student Teachers, brings to light a good number of new areas to be studied by future researchers. The areas and variables that are not covered by this study may be put to test to enlighten the other associated factors. So, the researchers may think of the following areas of study in detail:

1. This study can be extended to the students of all secondary school classes, intermediate, graduation and postgraduation at district and state levels;
2. Research studies may be undertaken to study the social intelligence of other professional courses like medicine, pharmacy, nursing, engineering, law, etc., as the very much interact with public;
3. Studies can be taken up on social intelligence linked with socio-economic status and other social and physical factors;

4. Studies can be undertaken to study the association of social intelligence with aptitude, attitude, personality, stress, conflicts, tensions, interests, motivation, mannerisms, etc.;
5. Studies can be undertaken to the family and public relationships in terms of social intelligence.

BIBLIOGRAPHY

Best, J.W. (1982). *Research in Education*. New Delhi: Prentice Hall of India Pvt. Ltd.

Byrne, R., and Whiten, A. (Eds.). (1988). *Machiavellian Intelligence: Social Expertise and the Evolution of Intellect in Monkeys, Apes, and Humans*. Oxford, U.K.: Clarendon Press.

Chauhan, S.S. (1978). *Advanced Educational Psychology*. New Delhi: Vikas Publishing House Pvt. Ltd.

Crow and Crow. *Educational Psychology*. New Delhi: S. Chand Co. Ltd.

Dash, M. and Neena Dash. (2006). *Fundamentals of Educational Psychology*. Delhi: Atlantic Publishers and Distributors.

Doll, E.A. (1947). *Social Maturity Scale*. Circle Pines, Mn.: American Guidance Service.

Ford, M.E., and Tisak, M.S. (1983). A Further Search for Social Intelligence. *Journal of Educational Psychology*, 75, 196-206.

Fredrickson, N., Carlson, S., and Ward, W.C. (1984). *The Place of Social Intelligence in a Taxonomy of Cognitive Abilities. Intelligence*, 8, 315-337.

Gallup, G.G. (1998). *Self-Awareness and the Evolution of Social Intelligence. Behavioural Processes*, 42, 239-247.

Goleman, D. (1995). *Emotional Intelligence, Why It Can Matter More Than IQ*. New York: Bantham Books.

Hoepfner, R., and O'Sullivan, M. *Social intelligence and IQ. Educational and Psychological Measurement*, 28, 339-344.

Hunt, T. (1928). *The Measurement of Social Intelligence. Journal of Applied Psychology,* 12, 317-334.

Kakkar, S. B. (1992). *Perspectives of Educational Psychology.* New Delhi: Atlantic Publishers and Distributors.

Keating, D.K. (1978). *A Search for Social Intelligence. Journal of Educational Psychology,* 70, 218-233.

Kihlstrom, J.F., and Cantor, N. (1989). *Social Intelligence and Personality*: There's Room for Growth. In R.S. Wyer and T.K. Srull Legree, P.J. (1995). Evidence for an Oblique Social Intelligence Factor Established with a Likert-based Testing Procedure. *Intelligence*, 21, 247-266.

Lokesh Koul. (1990). *Methodology of Educational Rcsearch.* New Delhi: Vikas Publishing House Pvt. Ltd.

Magotra, H.P. (1982). Mental Health as a Correlate of Intelligence, Education, Academic Achievement and Social Economic Status. In M.B. Buch, Editor. *The Third Survey of Research in Education.*

Manas Rajan, Panigrahi. (Oct. 2005). A Study on the Academic Achievement in Relation to Intelligence and Socio-economic Status of High School Students. *EduTracks*, Vol. 5, No. 1.

Mangal, S.K. (1979). Analysis of Common Factor in Teacher Adjustment. In M.B. Buch, Editor. *The Third Survey of Research in Education.*

Marlowe, H.A. (1986). Social Intelligence: Evidence for Multidimensionality and Construct Independence. *Journal of Educational Psychology,* 78, 52-58.

Marlowe, H.A., and Bedell, J.R. (1982). Social Intelligence: Evidence for Independence of the Construct. *Psychological Reports*, 51, 461-462.

Moss, F.A. (1931). Preliminary Report of a Study of Social Intelligence and Executive Ability. *Public Personnel Studies*, 9, 2-9.

Moss, F.A., and Hunt, T. (1927). Are you Socially Intelligent? *Scientific American,* 137, 108-110.

Moss, F.A., Hunt, T., Omwake, K.T., and Ronning, M.M. (1927). *Social Intelligence Test.* Washington, D.C.: Center for Psychological Service.

Moss, F.A., Hunt, T., Omwake, K.T., and Woodward, L.G. (1955). *Manual for the George Washington University Series Social Intelligence Test.* Washington, D.C.: Center for Psychological Service.

Murthy, S. K. (1983). *Teacher Education in Indian Society.* Ludhiana: Educational Publishers.

Nanda, S.K. *Educational Psychology*. Jalandhar: New Academic Publishers Company.

O'Sullivan, M., Guilford, J.P., and deMille, R. (1965). The Measurement of Social Intelligence. *Reports from the Psychological Laboratory, University of Southern California,* No. 34.

Pathak, R.D. (1978). Sociometric Status and Adjustment Level in School Children. In M.B. Buch, Editor. *The Third Survey of Research in Education.*

Ram Nath, Sharma and Sharma, R. K. (2003). *Advanced Educational Psychology*. Delhi: Atlantic Publishers and Distributors.

Saovaluk Thoungngamhom. (1983). A Study of Social Maturity as a Function of Some Psycho-Socio Adjustment Factors of B.Ed. Colleges Students of North Central Region of Thailand. In M. B. Buch, Editor. The Fourth Survey of Research in Education.

Saravanavel, P. (1991). *Research Methodology.*

Sechrest, L., and Jackson, D.N. (1961). Social Intelligence and the Accuracy of Interpersonal Predictions. *Journal of Personality*, 29, 167-182.

Shanley, L.A., Walker, R.E., and Foley, J.M. (1971). Social Intelligence: A Concept in Search of Data. *Psychological Reports*, 29, 1123-1132.

Sharma, R.A. *Teacher Education*. Meerut: International Publishing.

Sidhu, K.S. *Methodology of Research in Education*. New Delhi: Sterling Publishers Pvt. Ltd.

Sipps, G.J., Berry, G.W., and Lynch, E.M. (1987). WAIS-R and Social Intelligence: A Test of Established Assumptions that Uses the CPI. *Journal of Clinical Psychology*, 43, 499-504.

Sternberg, R.J., and Smith, C. (1985). Social Intelligence and Decoding Skills in Non-verbal Communication. *Social Cognition*, 3, 168-192.

Sukhia, S. P., Mehrotra, P.V. and Mehrotra, R.N. (1991). *Elements of Educational Research*. New Delhi: Allied Publishers Pvt. Ltd.

Taylor, E.H. (1990). *The Assessment of Social Intelligence*. Psychotherapy, 27, 445-457.

Taylor, E.H., and Cadet, J.L. (1989). *Social Intelligence, a Neurological System? Psychological Reports*, 64, 423-444.

Thorndike, R.L. (1936). Factor Analysis of Social and Abstract Intelligence. *Journal of Educational Psychology*, 27, 231-233.

Vatsyayan. (1984). *Social Psychology*.

Vora, J. I. (1980). Social Maturity of Students of College of Education in the Context of Some Psycho-socio Correlates. In M.B. Buch, Editor. *The Third Survey of Research in Education*.

Walker, R.E., and Foley, J.M. (1973). Social Intelligence: Its History and Measurement. *Psychological Reports*, 33, 839-864.

Wong, C.-M. T., Day, J.D., Maxwell, S.E., and Meara, N.M. (1995). A Multitrait-multimethod Study of Academic and Social Intelligence in College Students. *Journal of Educational Psychology*, 87, 117-133.

Worden, R.P. (1996). Primate Social Intelligence. *Cognitive Science*, 20, 579-616.

Additional References

Bhaskara Rao, Digumarti (1994). *Scientific Aptitude*. New Delhi: Ashish Publishing House. ISBN 81-7024-658-X.

Bhaskara Rao, Digumarti (1995). *Animal Kingdom*. New Delhi: Discovery Publishing House. ISBN 81-7141-274-2.

Bhaskara Rao, Digumarti (1995). *Batracology*. New Delhi: Discovery Publishing House. ISBN 81-7141-279-3.

Bhaskara Rao, Digumarti (1997). *Scientific Attitude*. New Delhi: Discovery Publishing House. ISBN 81-7141-381-1.

Bhaskara Rao, Digumarti (1996). *Scientific Attitude vis-à-vis Scientific Aptitude*. New Delhi: Discovery Publishing House. ISBN 81-7141-308-0.

Bhaskara Rao, Digumarti (2004). *Scientific Attitude, Scientific Aptitude and Achievement*. New Delhi: Discovery Publishing House. ISBN 81-7141-781-7.

Bhaskara Rao, Digumarti (2004). *Educational Administration*. New Delhi: Discovery Publishing House. ISBN 81-7141-842-2.

Bhaskara Rao, Digumarti (2004). *Issues in School Education*. New Delhi: Discovery Publishing House. ISBN 81-8356-025-3.

Bhaskara Rao, Digumarti, Editor (1996). *Encyclopaedia of Education For All*, 5 Volumes. New Delhi: APH Publishing Corporation. ISBN 81-7024-759-4 (set).

Vol. I *Education For All: The World Conference*. ISBN 81-7024-760-8.

Vol. II *Education For All: The EPA-9 Summit*. ISBN 81-7024-761-6.

Vol. III *Education For All: Quality Education For All*. ISBN 81-7024-762-6.

Vol. IV *Education For All: Planning and Monitoring.* ISBN 81-7024-763-4.

Vol. V *Education For All: The Indian Scenario.* ISBN 81-7024-764-0.

Bhaskara Rao, Digumarti, Editor (1996). *National Policy on Education*, 2 Volumes. New Delhi: Anmol Publications Pvt. Ltd. ISBN 81-7488-323-1.

Bhaskara Rao, Digumarti, Editor (1996). *Global Perceptions on Peace Education*, 3 Volumes. New Delhi: Discovery Publishing House. ISBN 81-7141-319-6.

Bhaskara Rao, Digumarti, Editor (1997). *Education for the 21st Century.* New Delhi: Discovery Publishing House. ISBN 81-7141-389-7.

Bhaskara Rao, Digumarti, Editor (1997). *Reflections on Scientific Attitude.* New Delhi: Discovery Publishing House. ISBN 81-7141-319-6.

Bhaskara Rao, Digumarti, Editor (1997). *Success Story of a Primary Education Project.* New Delhi: APH Publishing Corporation. ISBN 81-7024-850-7.

Bhaskara Rao, Digumarti, Editor (1997). *World Food Summit.* New Delhi: Discovery Publishing House. ISBN 81-7141-386-2.

Bhaskara Rao, Digumarti, Editor (1997). *Care the Child*, 2 Volumes. New Delhi: Discovery Publishing House. ISBN 81-7141-394-3.

Bhaskara Rao, Digumarti, Editor (1998). *Earth Summit*, 2 Volumes. New Delhi: Discovery Publishing House. ISBN 81-7141-435-4.

Bhaskara Rao, Digumarti, Editor (1998). *Adolescence Education.* New Delhi: Discovery Publishing House. ISBN 81-7141-432-X.

Bhaskara Rao, Digumarti, Editor (1998). *Community and School Nutrition Education.* New Delhi: Discovery Publishing House. ISBN 81-7141-435-4.

Bhaskara Rao, Digumarti, Editor (1998). *District Primary Education Programme*. New Delhi: Discovery Publishing House. ISBN 81-7141-396-X.

Bhaskara Rao, Digumarti, Editor (1998). *National Policy on Education: Towards An Enlightened and Humane Society*. New Delhi: Discovery Publishing House. ISBN 81-7141-426-5.

Bhaskara Rao, Digumarti, Editor (1998). *Reforming School Education*. New Delhi: Discovery Publishing House. ISBN 81-7141-403-6.

Bhaskara Rao, Digumarti, Editor (1998). *Teacher Education in India*. New Delhi: Discovery Publishing House. ISBN 81-7141-406-0.

Bhaskara Rao, Digumarti, Editor (1998). *World Summit for Social Development*. New Delhi: Discovery Publishing House. ISBN 81-7141-420-6.

Bhaskara Rao, Digumarti, Editor (1999). *International Encyclopaedia of AIDS*, 11 Volumes. New Delhi: Discovery Publishing House. ISBN 81-7141-522-6 (set).

Vol. 1 *Introduction to HIV/AIDS*. ISBN 81-7141-523-7.

Vol. 2 HIV/AIDS – Issues and Challenges, 2 Parts. ISBN 81-7141-524-5.

Vol. 3 *HIV/AIDS – Socio-economic Realities*. ISBN 81-7141-524-3.

Vol. 4 *HIV/AIDS – Law Ethics and Human Rights*, 2 Parts. ISBN 81-7141-526-1.

Vol. 5 *AIDS and NGOs*. ISBN 81-7141-527-X.

Vol. 6 *AIDS and Home Care*. ISBN 81-7141-528-8.

Vol. 7 *STD Case Management*. ISBN 81-7141-529-6.

Vol. 8 *HIV/AIDS Prevention and Care – Teaching Modules for Nurses and Midwives*. ISBN 81-7141-530-X.

Vol. 9 *HIV Prevention Education for Educational Institutions.* ISBN 81-7141-531-8.

Vol. 10 *Instructional Modules for AIDS Education.* ISBN 81-7141-532-6.

Vol. 11 *School Health Education to Prevent AIDS and STD – A Package for Curriculum Planners.* ISBN 81-7141-533-4.

Bhaskara Rao, Digumarti, Editor (2000). *International Encyclopaedia of Human Rights*, 7 Volumes in 13 Parts. New Delhi: Discovery Publishing House. ISBN 81-7141-567-9 (set).

Vol. 1 *International Instruments of Human Rights,* 2 Parts. ISBN 81-7141-569-4.

Vol. 2 *Regional Instruments of Human Rights.* ISBN 81-7141-604-7.

Vol. 3 *Human Rights and the United Nations,* 2 Parts. ISBN 81-7141-605-5.

Vol. 4 *Fact Files of Human Rights,* 3 Parts. ISBN 81-7141-606-3.

Vol. 5 *Study Stories of Human Rights,* 3 Parts. ISBN 81-7141-607-3.

Vol. 6 *International Meetings on Human Rights,* 2 Parts. ISBN 81-7141-608-X.

Vol. 7 *Professional Training in Human Rights.* ISBN 81-7141-609-8.

Bhaskara Rao, Digumarti, Editor (2000). *International Encyclopaedia of Science and Technology Education,* 11 Volumes. New Delhi: Discovery Publishing House. ISBN 81-7141-548-2 (set).

Vol. 1 *Science and Technology Education.* ISBN 81-7141-568-7.

Vol. 2 *Science Education in Developing Countries.* ISBN 81-7141-569-9.

Vol. 3 *Organizational Structure of Science.* ISBN 81-7141-570-9.

Vol. 4 *Science Education in Asia and the Pacific.* ISBN 81-7141-571-7.

Vol. 5 *Science and Technology Education For All.* ISBN 81-7141-572-5.

Vol. 6 *Values, Ethics, Talent and Girls in Science and Technology Education.* ISBN 81-7141-573-3.

Vol. 7 *Popularisation of Science and Technology Education.* ISBN 81-7141-574-1.

Vol. 8 *Science, Power and Society.* ISBN 81-7141-575-X.

Vol. 9 *Information Technology.* ISBN 81-7141-576-8.

Vol. 10 *Teacher Training in Science and Technology Education.* ISBN 81-7141-577-6.

Vol. 11 *Teacher Training in Science and Technology: A Curriculum Framework.* ISBN 81-7141-578-4.

Bhaskara Rao, Digumarti, Editor (2000). *Education For All: Achieving the Goal,* 3 Volumes. New Delhi: APH Publishing Corporation. ISBN 81-7648-152-1 (set).

Vol. I *The Global Consensus.* ISBN 81-7648-155-6.

Vol. II *Mid-Decade Review Reports of Regional Seminars.* ISBN 81-7648- 154-8.

Vol. III *Issues and Trends.* ISBN 81-7648-155-6.

Bhaskara Rao, Digumarti, Editor (2001). *Nuclear Materials: Issues and Concerns,* 2 Volumes. New Delhi: Discovery Publishing House. ISBN 81-7141-611-X.

Bhaskara Rao, Digumarti, Editor (2001). *Distance Education in Different Countries.* New Delhi: APH Publishing Corporation. ISBN 81-7648-229-3.

Bhaskara Rao, Digumarti, Editor (2001). *Decentralised Management of Education: Management of Education in Panchayati Raj and Municipal Bodies.* New Delhi: Discovery Publishing House. ISBN 81-7141-617-9.

Bhaskara Rao, Digumarti, Editor (2001). *Electrochemistry for Environmental Protection*. New Delhi: Discovery Publishing House. ISBN 81-7141-619-5.

Bhaskara Rao, Digumarti, Editor (2001). *Global Educational Studies*. New Delhi: Discovery Publishing House. ISBN 81-7141-616-0.

Bhaskara Rao, Digumarti, Editor (2001). *Global Synthesis of Educational Assessment*. New Delhi: Discovery Publishing House. ISBN 81-7141-613-6.

Bhaskara Rao, Digumarti, Editor (2001). *Jomtein Decade of Education*. New Delhi: Discovery Publishing House. ISBN 81-7141-618-7.

Bhaskara Rao, Digumarti, Editor (2001). *World Conference on Education for All*. New Delhi: Discovery Publishing House. ISBN 81-7141-274-9.

Bhaskara Rao, Digumarti, Editor (2001). *World Conference on Higher Education*. New Delhi: Discovery Publishing House. ISBN 81-7141-610-1.

Bhaskara Rao, Digumarti, Editor (2001). *World Conference on Science*. New Delhi: Discovery Publishing House. ISBN 81-7141-612-8.

Bhaskara Rao, Digumarti, Editor (2003). *Inspiring Experiences in Teacher Education*. New Delhi: Discovery Publishing House. ISBN 81-7141-656-X.

Bhaskara Rao, Digumarti, Editor (2003). *International Studies in Education*, 3 Volumes. New Delhi: Discovery Publishing House. ISBN 81-7141-647-0.

Bhaskara Rao, Digumarti, Editor (2003). *Military Conversion: Impact on Science and Technology*. New Delhi: Discovery Publishing House. ISBN 81-7141-578-4.

Bhaskara Rao, Digumarti, Editor (2003). *United Nations Millennium Summit*. New Delhi: Discovery Publishing House. ISBN 81-7141-632-2.

Bhaskara Rao, Digumarti, Editor (2003). *World Assembly on Aging*. New Delhi: Discovery Publishing House. ISBN 81-7141-637-3.

Bhaskara Rao, Digumarti, Editor (2003). *World Conference on Human Rights.* New Delhi: Discovery Publishing House. ISBN 81-7141-661-6.

Bhaskara Rao, Digumarti, Editor (2003). *World Education Forum.* New Delhi: Discovery Publishing House. ISBN 81-7141-639-X.

Bhaskara Rao, Digumarti, Editor (2003). *Education, Employment and Human Resource Development.* New Delhi: Discovery Publishing House. ISBN 81-7141-681-0.

Bhaskara Rao, Digumarti, Editor (2003). *Successful Schooling.* New Delhi: Discovery Publishing House. ISBN 81-7141-677-2.

Bhaskara Rao, Digumarti, Editor (2003). *European Education and Teachers.* New Delhi: Discovery Publishing House. ISBN 81-7141-702-7.

Bhaskara Rao, Digumarti, Editor (2003). *Teachers in a Changing World.* New Delhi: Discovery Publishing House. ISBN 81-7141-694-2.

Bhaskara Rao, Digumarti, Editor (2004). *International Guidelines on Open and Distance Teacher Education.* New Delhi: Discovery Publishing House. ISBN 81-7141-777-9.

Bhaskara Rao, Digumarti, Editor (2004). *Adult Learning in the 21st Century.* New Delhi: Discovery Publishing House. ISBN 81-7141-797-3.

Bhaskara Rao, Digumarti, Editor (2004). *Educational Practices: Research and Recommendations.* New Delhi: Discovery Publishing House. ISBN 81-7141-835-X.

Bhaskara Rao, Digumarti, Editor (2004). *General Secondary Education In the 21st Century.* New Delhi: Discovery Publishing House. ISBN 81-7141-885-6.

Bhaskara Rao, Digumarti, Editor (2004). *International Encyclopaedia of Learning to Live Together*, 4 Volumes. New Delhi: Discovery Publishing House. ISBN 81-7141-848-1.

Vol. 1 *International Conference on Learning to Live Together.*

Vol. 2 *Globalisation and Living Together.*

Vol. 3 *Curriculum for Learning to Live Together.*

Vol. 4 *Science Education for the Contemporary Society.*

Bhaskara Rao, Digumarti, Editor (2004). *Reforming Secondary Education.* New Delhi: Discovery Publishing House. ISBN 81-7141-843-0.

Bhaskara Rao, Digumarti, Editor (2004). *Human Rights Education.* New Delhi: Discovery Publishing House. ISBN 81-7141-882-1.

Bhaskara Rao, Digumarti, Editor (2004). *United Nations Decade for Human Rights Education.* New Delhi: Discovery Publishing House. ISBN 81-7141-887-2.

Bhaskara Rao, Digumarti, Editor (2004). *Technical and Vocational Education and Training in the 21st Century.* New Delhi: Discovery Publishing House. ISBN 81-7141- 984-4.

Bhaskara Rao, Digumarti, Editor (2005). *Encyclopaedia of Education For All,* 5 Volumes. New Delhi: Discovery Publishing House.

Bhaskara Rao, Digumarti and B.S.V. Dutt, Editors (2003). *Education: Programmes and Policies.* New Delhi: APH Publishing Corporation. ISBN 81-7648-470-9.

Bhaskara Rao, Digumarti, C.A.P. Swamy and B.S.V. Dutt (1997). *Self-Evaluation in Student Teaching.* New Delhi: Discovery Publishing House. ISBN 81-7141-374-9.

Bhaskara Rao, Digumarti and D. Naresh Kumar (2004). *School Teacher Effectiveness.* New Delhi: Discovery Publishing House. ISBN 81-7141-782-5.

Bhaskara Rao, Digumarti and D. Sridhar (2002). *Job Satisfaction of School Teachers.* New Delhi: Discovery Publishing House. ISBN 81-7141-652-7.

Bhaskara Rao, Digumarti, C. Sridevi and K. Vijaya (1995). *Achievement in Social Studies.* New Delhi: Discovery Publishing House. ISBN 81-7141-281-5.

Bhaskara Rao, Digumarti and Digumarti Pushpa Latha (1994). *Achievement in Biology*. New Delhi: Discovery Publishing House. ISBN 81-7141-264-5.

Bhaskara Rao, Digumarti and Digumarti Pushpa Latha (1995). *Achievement in English*. New Delhi: Discovery Publishing House. ISBN 81-7141-283-1.

Bhaskara Rao, Digumarti and Digumarti Pushpa Latha (1994). *Achievement in Science*. New Delhi: Discovery Publishing House. ISBN 81-7141-280-70.

Bhaskara Rao, Digumarti and Digumarti Pushpa Latha (1995). *Achievement in Mathematics*. New Delhi: Discovery Publishing House. ISBN 81-7141-278-5.

Bhaskara Rao, Digumarti and Digumarti Pushpa Latha (2004). *Education for Women*. New Delhi: Discovery Publishing House. ISBN 81-7141-873-2.

Bhaskara Rao, Digumarti, Digumarti Pushpa Latha and Digumarthi Harshitha, Editors (2001). *Biological Warfare*. New Delhi: Discovery Publishing House. ISBN 81-7141-597-0.

Bhaskara Rao, Digumarti, Digumarti Pushpa Latha and Digumarthi Harshitha, Editors (2001). *Women as Educators*. New Delhi: Discovery Publishing House. ISBN 81-7141-602-0.

Bhaskara Rao, Digumarti and Digumarthi Harshitha (2004). *Adjustment of Adolescents*. New Delhi: APH Publishing House. ISBN 81-7648-836-8.

Bhaskara Rao, Digumarti and Digumarthi Harshitha, Editors (2001). *Education in India*. New Delhi: APH Publishing House. ISBN 81-7648-207-2.

Bhaskara Rao, Digumarti and Digumarti Pushpa Latha, Editors (1998). *International Encyclopaedia of Women*, 5 volumes. New Delhi: Discovery Publishing House. ISBN 81-7141-410-9 (set).

Vol. 1 *Status of World's Women.* ISBN 81-7141-494-X.

Vol. 2 *Women, Education and Empowerment.* ISBN 81-7141-498-1.

Vol. 3 *Women Challenges and Advancement.* ISBN 81-7141-497-4.

Vol. 4 *Women and Family Health.* ISBN 81-7141-497-4.

Vol. 5 *Women and International Action.* ISBN 81-7141-498-2.

Bhaskara Rao, Digumarti, Digumarti Pushpa Latha and Digumarthi Harshitha, Editors (2001). *Assessing Learning Achievement.* New Delhi: Discovery Publishing House. ISBN 81-7141-601-2.

Bhaskara Rao, Digumarti, Digumarti Pushpa Latha and Digumarthi Harshitha, Editors (2001). *Energy Security.* New Delhi: Discovery Publishing House. ISBN 81-7141-598-9.

Bhaskara Rao, Digumarti, Digumarthi Harshitha and K.R.S. Sambasiva Rao, Editors (1999). *Advanced Biotechnology.* New Delhi: Discovery Publishing House. ISBN 81-7141-516-4.

Bhaskara Rao, Digumarti and K.R.S. Sambasiva Rao, Editors (1996). *Current Trends in Indian Education.* New Delhi: Discovery Publishing House. ISBN 81-7141-311-0.

Bhaskara Rao, Digumarti and D. Naresh Kumar (2004). *School Teacher Effectiveness.* New Delhi: Discovery Publishing House. ISBN 81-7141-782-5.

Bhaskara Rao, Digumarti and E. Sreekanth Babu (2004). *Educational Interests of School Students.* New Delhi: Discovery Publishing House. ISBN 81-7141-837-6.

Bhaskara Rao, Digumarti and K. Vijaya (1995). *A Text Book Evaluation.* Ambala Cantt: The Associated Publishers.

Bhaskara Rao, Digumarti and M.A. Fayaz (2004). *Problems of Primary School Drop-outs.* New Delhi: Discovery Publishing House. ISBN 81-7141- 834-1.

Bhaskara Rao, Digumarti and N.V.M. Mohana Rao (2002). *Problems of Mentally Handicapped Children.* New Delhi: Discovery Publishing House. ISBN 81-7141-645-4.

Bhaskara Rao, Digumarti and S. Chandra Mohan (2002). *Sports Management.* New Delhi: APH Publishing House. ISBN 81-7648-467-9.

Bhaskara Rao, Digumarti and S.A. Khader (2004). *Problems of Private School Teachers.* New Delhi: Discovery Publishing Corporation. ISBN 81-7141-838-4.

Bhaskara Rao, Digumarti and S.A. Khader (2004). *School Education in India.* New Delhi: Discovery Publishing House. ISBN 81-7141-849-X.

Bhaskara Rao, Digumarti and Sk. Johni Basha (2004). *Teachers' Population Education Awareness.* New Delhi: Discovery Publishing House. ISBN 81-7141-832-5.

Bhaskara Rao, Digumarti, V.V. Rao, V.V. Lakshmi and V.V. Krishna, Editors (1999). *Status and Advancement of Women.* New Delhi: APH Publishing Corporation. ISBN 81-7648-169-6.

Appala Naidu, P.Ch., Author and Digumarti Bhaskara Rao, Editor (2007). *Feedback Methods and Students Performance.* New Delhi: Discovery Publishing House. ISBN 81-8356-284-1.

Babu, P.C., Author and Digumarti Bhaskara Rao, Editor (2004). *Flowers of Wisdom.* New Delhi: Discovery Publishing House. ISBN 81-7141-695-0.

Babu, P.C., Author and Digumarti Bhaskara Rao, Editor (2008). *Worlds of Wisdom.* New Delhi: Discovery Publishing House.

Bujji Babu, K., Author and Digumarti Bhaskara Rao, Editor (2007). *Teaching Aptitude of Primary School Teachers.* New Delhi: Sonali Publications. ISBN 81-8411-083-9.

Amala, P. A. and Anupama, P., Authors and Digumarti Bhaskara Rao, Editor (2004). *History of Education.* New Delhi: Discovery Publishing House. ISBN 81-7141-860-0.

Bhagya Lakshmi, L., Author and Digumarti Bhaskara Rao, Editor (2000). *Reading and Comprehension.* New Delhi: Discovery Publishing House. ISBN 81-7141-543-1.

Bhasha, S.A., Author and Digumarti Bhaskara Rao, Editor (2004). *Methods of Teaching Geography.* New Delhi: Discovery Publishing House. ISBN 81-7141-807-4.

Bhuvaneswara Lakshmi, Gadde, Author and Digumarti Bhaskara Rao, Editor (2000). *Attitude Towards Science.* New Delhi: Discovery Publishing House. ISBN 81-7141-541-6.

Bhuvaneswara Lakshmi, G., Author and Digumarti Bhaskara Rao, Editor (2004). *Methods of Teaching Life Science.* New Delhi: Discovery Publishing House. ISBN 81-7141-804-X.

Bhuvaneswara Lakshmi, G. and K. Subba Rao, Authors and Digumarti Bhaskara Rao, Editor (2004). *Methods of Teaching Biology.* New Delhi: Discovery Publishing House. ISBN 81-7141-914-3.

Bramhaiah, T., Author and Digumarti Bhaskara Rao, Editor (2008). *Stress of Prospective Teachers.* New Delhi: Sonali Publications.

Chary, K.V.N.B., Author and Digumarti Bhaskara Rao, Editor (2006). *Techniques of Teaching Physics.* New Delhi: Sonali Publications. ISBN 81-8411-046-4.

Chowdary, S.B.J.R. and Naga Raju, Authors and Digumarti Bhaskara Rao, Editor (2004). *Mastery of Teaching Skills.* New Delhi: Discovery Publishing House. ISBN 81-7141-861-9.

Dayakara Reddy, V. and Digumarti Bhaskara Rao, Editors (2006). *Value-oriented Education.* New Delhi: Discovery Publishing House. ISBN 81-8356-051-2.

Devraj, T.A.S., Author and Digumarti Bhaskara Rao, Editor (1997). *Trace Analysis of Uranium and Thorium.* New Delhi: Discovery Publishing House. ISBN 81-7141-375-7.

Durga Rani, K., Author and Digumarti Bhaskara Rao, Editor (2000). *Educational Aspirations and Scientific Attitudes.* New Delhi: Discovery Publishing House. ISBN 81-7141-555-5.

Dutt, B.S.V. and Digumarti Bhaskara Rao (2001). *Empowering Primary Teachers.* New Delhi: Discovery Publishing House. ISBN 81-7141-615-2.

Dutt, B.S.V., Author and Digumarti Bhaskara Rao, Editor (2004). *Comparative Education.* New Delhi: Discovery Publishing House. ISBN 81-7141-912-7.

Ediger, Marlow and Digumarti Bhaskara Rao (1996). *Science Curriculum.* New Delhi: Discovery Publishing House. ISBN 81-7141-321-8.

Ediger, Marlow and Digumarti Bhaskara Rao (2000). *Teaching Mathematics Successfully.* New Delhi: Discovery Publishing House. ISBN 81-7141-552-0.

Ediger, Marlow and Digumarti Bhaskara Rao (2001). *Teaching Science Successfully.* New Delhi: Discovery Publishing House. ISBN 81-7141-600-4.

Ediger, Marlow and Digumarti Bhaskara Rao (2001). *Teaching Social Studies Successfully.* New Delhi: Discovery Publishing House. ISBN 81-7141-596-2.

Ediger, Marlow and Digumarti Bhaskara Rao (2002). *Philosophy and Curriculum.* New Delhi: Discovery Publishing House. ISBN 81-7141-631-4.

Ediger, Marlow and Digumarti Bhaskara Rao (2002). *Improving School Administration.* New Delhi: Discovery Publishing House. ISBN 81-7141-633-0.

Ediger, Marlow and Digumarti Bhaskara Rao (2002). *Elementary Curriculum.* New Delhi: Discovery Publishing House. ISBN 81-7141-658-6.

Ediger, Marlow and Digumarti Bhaskara Rao (2003). *Language Arts Curriculum.* New Delhi: Discovery Publishing House. ISBN 81-7141-657-8.

Ediger, Marlow and Digumarti Bhaskara Rao (2003). *Psychology and Curriculum*. New Delhi: Discovery Publishing House. ISBN 81-7141-691-8.

Ediger, Marlow and Digumarti Bhaskara Rao (2003). *Teaching Language Arts Successfully*. New Delhi: Discovery Publishing House. ISBN 81-7141-678-0.

Ediger, Marlow and Digumarti Bhaskara Rao (2003). *School Curriculum and Administration*. New Delhi: Discovery Publishing House. ISBN 81-7141-709-4.

Ediger, Marlow and Digumarti Bhaskara Rao (2003). *Teaching Mathematics in Elementary Schools*. New Delhi: Discovery Publishing House. ISBN 81-7141-687-X.

Ediger, Marlow and Digumarti Bhaskara Rao (2003). *Teaching Science in Elementary Schools*. New Delhi: Discovery Publishing House. ISBN 81-7141-698-5.

Ediger, Marlow and Digumarti Bhaskara Rao (2003). *School Curriculum and Administration*. New Delhi: Discovery Publishing House. ISBN 81-7141-709-4.

Ediger, Marlow and Digumarti Bhaskara Rao (2003). *Elementary Curriculum Improvement*. New Delhi: Discovery Publishing House. ISBN 81-7141-740-X.

Ediger, Marlow and Digumarti Bhaskara Rao (2004). *School Organisation*. New Delhi: Discovery Publishing House. ISBN 81-7141-843-0.

Ediger, Marlow and Digumarti Bhaskara Rao (2004). *Relevancy in Elementary Curriculum*. New Delhi: Discovery Publishing House. ISBN 81-7141-845-9.

Ediger, Marlow and Digumarti Bhaskara Rao (2005). *Quality School Education*. New Delhi: Discovery Publishing House. ISBN 81-8356-022-9.

Ediger, Marlow and Digumarti Bhaskara Rao (2006). *Successful School Education*. New Delhi: Discovery Publishing House. ISBN 81-8356-054-7.

Ediger, Marlow and Digumarti Bhaskara Rao (2006). *Successful School Administration.* New Delhi: Discovery Publishing House. ISBN 81-8356-046-6.

Ediger, Marlow and Digumarti Bhaskara Rao (2006). *Issues in School Curriculum.* New Delhi: Discovery Publishing House. ISBN 81-8356-052-0.

Ediger, Marlow and Digumarti Bhaskara Rao (2006). *Community College – Curriculum and Teaching.* New Delhi: Discovery Publishing House. ISBN 81-8356-053-9.

Ediger, Marlow and Digumarti Bhaskara Rao (2006). *Administration of Schools.* New Delhi: Discovery Publishing House. ISBN 81-8356-244-2.

Ediger, Marlow and Digumarti Bhaskara Rao (2006). *Reading Curriculum and Instruction.* New Delhi: Discovery Publishing House. ISBN 81-8356-266-3.

Ediger, Marlow and Digumarti Bhaskara Rao (2006). *Curriculum Organisation.* New Delhi: Discovery Publishing House. ISBN 81-8356-205-1.

Ediger, Marlow and Digumarti Bhaskara Rao (2006). *Curriculum of School Subjects.* New Delhi: Discovery Publishing House. ISBN 81-8356-207-8.

Ediger, Marlow, B.S.V. Dutt and Digumarti Bhaskara Rao (2003). *Teaching English Successfully.* New Delhi: Discovery Publishing House. ISBN 81-7141-707-8.

Ediger, Marlow and Digumarti Bhaskara Rao (2007). *School Science Education.* New Delhi: Discovery Publishing House. ISBN 81-8356-352-X.

Ediger, Marlow and Digumarti Bhaskara Rao (2007). *Language Arts Education.* New Delhi: Discovery Publishing House. ISBN 81-8356-333-3.

Elizabeth, M.E.S., Author and Digumarti Bhaskara Rao, Editor (2004). *Methods of Teaching English.* New Delhi: Discovery Publishing House. ISBN 81-7141-809-0.

Elizabeth, M.E.S., Author and Digumarti Bhaskara Rao, Editor (2004). *Acquisition of English Vocabulary*. New Delhi: Discovery Publishing House. ISBN 81-8356-075-X.

Fatima, Sk. Author and Digumarti Bhaskara Rao, Editor (2007). *Reasoning Ability of School Students*. New Delhi: Discovery Publishing House. ISBN 81-8356-330-9.

Fatima, Sk. and Digumarti Bhaskara Rao (2008). *Reasoning Ability of Adolescent Students*. New Delhi: Discovery Publishing House Pvt. Ltd. ISBN 978-81-8356-315-4.

Gopala Krishna, M., Author and Digumarti Bhaskara Rao, Editor (2007). *Techniques of Teaching Physical Education*. New Delhi: Sonali Publications. ISBN 81-8411-044-8.

Gopala Krishna, M., Author and Digumarti Bhaskara Rao, Editor (2007). *Techniques of Teaching Education*. New Delhi: Sonali Publications. ISBN 81-8411-062-6.

Harshitha, Digumarthi, Author and Digumarti Bhaskara Rao, Editor (2004). *Methods of Teaching Information Technology*. New Delhi: Discovery Publishing House. ISBN 81-7141-805-8.

Harshitha, Digumarthi, Author and Digumarti Bhaskara Rao, Editor (2007). *Techniques of Teaching Computer Science*. New Delhi: Sonali Publications. ISBN 81-8411-036-7.

Indira Devi, Author and J. Prasanth Kumar and Digumarti Bhaskara Rao, Editors (2004). *Values in Language Text Books*. New Delhi: Discovery Publishing House. ISBN 81-7141-833-3.

Jalaja Kumari, C., Author and Digumarti Bhaskara Rao, Editor (2004). *Methods of Teaching Educational Technology*. New Delhi: Discovery Publishing House. ISBN 81-7141-810-4.

Jalaja Kumari, C., Author and Digumarti Bhaskara Rao, Editor (2007). *Job Satisfaction of Teachers*. New Delhi: Discovery Publishing House. ISBN 81-8356-329-5.

Janardhan Reddy, B., Author and Digumarti Bhaskara Rao, Editor (2006). *Techniques of Teaching Sociology*. New Delhi: Sonali Publications. ISBN 81-8411-042-1.

Jayalakshmi, M., Author and Digumarti Bhaskara Rao, Editor (2009). *Microteaching and Prospective Teachers*. New Delhi: Discovery Publishing House.

Jayasree, K., Author and Digumarti Bhaskara Rao, Editor (1999). *Correlates of Socialisaiion*. New Delhi: Discovery Publishing House. ISBN 81-7141-517-2.

Jayasree, K., Author and Digumarti Bhaskara Rao, Editor (2004). *Methods of Teaching Science*. New Delhi: Discovery Publishing House. ISBN 81-7141-801-5.

John Babu, C., Author and T.J.R. Prasad, G.M. Madhukar and Digumarti Bhaskara Rao, Editors (2004). *Problem Solving in Mathematics*. New Delhi: APH Publishing Corporation. ISBN 81-7648-273-0.

Joseph Raju, B and G.A. Anitha, authors and Digumarti Bhaskara Rao, Editor (2004). *Population Education*. New Delhi: Sonali Publications. ISBN 81-88836-31-3.

Lalitha, T., Author and K.S. Prabhakaram, D.S.N. Sastry and Digumarti Bhaskara Rao, Editors (2004). *Educational Philosophic Beliefs*. New Delhi: Discovery Publishing House. ISBN 81-7141-765-5.

Krishna, G., Author and Digumarti Bhaskara Rao, Editor (2006). *Techniques of Teaching Physical Education*. New Delhi: Sonali Publications. ISBN 81-8411-044-8.

Kumar Raja, G., Author and Digumarti Bhaskara Rao, Editor (2007). *Principles of Primary School*. New Delhi: Sonali Publications. ISBN 81-8411-054-5.

Lakshmi Kumari, V., Author and Digumarti Bhaskara Rao, Editor (2006). *Techniques of Teaching Home Science*. New Delhi: Sonali Publications. ISBN 81-8411-048-0.

Madhava, K., Author and Digumarti Bhaskara Rao, Editor (2008). *Personality of Adolescent Students*. New Delhi: Discovery Publishing House. ISBN 978-81-8356-262-1.

Madhu Bala, Jampala, Author and Digumarti Bhaskara Rao, Editor (2004). *Methods of Teaching Exceptional Children*. New Delhi: Discovery Publishing House. ISBN 81-7141-802-3.

Madhu Bala, Jampala, Author and Digumarti Bhaskara Rao, Editor (2007). *Adjustment, Problems of Hearing Impaired.* New Delhi: Discovery Publishing House. ISBN 81-7141-831-7.

Marja, Talvi and Digumarti Bhaskara Rao, Editors (1996). *Educational Leadership and Social Changes.* New Delhi: Discovery Publishing House. ISBN 81-7141-320-X.

Mohana Sundari, C., Author and B. Prasad Babu and Digumarti Bhaskara Rao, Editors (2008). *Stress Among Pregnant Women.* New Delhi: Discovery Publishing House Pvt. Ltd. ISBN 978-81-8356-316-1.

Naga Kumari, U., Author and Digumarti Bhaskara Rao, Editor (2008). *Science Process Skills of School Students.* New Delhi: Discovery Publishing House Pvt. Ltd. ISBN 978-81-8356-263-8.

Nageswara Rao, S. and M. Srihari, Authors and Digumarti Bhaskara Rao, Editor (2004). *Guidance and Counselling.* New Delhi: Discovery Publishing House. ISBN 81-7141-840-6.

Nageswara Rao, S., Author and Digumarti Bhaskara Rao, Editor (2006). *Techniques of Teaching Psychology.* New Delhi: Sonali Publications. ISBN 81-8411-040-5.

Nageswara Rao, S. and P. Sridhar, Authors and Digumarti Bhaskara Rao, Editor (2004). *Methods and Techniques of Teaching.* New Delhi: Sonali Publications. ISBN 81-88836-33-8.

Nirmala Jyothi, M., Author and Digumarti Bhaskara Rao, Editor (2003). *Non-detention System in School Education.* New Delhi: Discovery Publishing House. ISBN 81-7141-654-3.

Padma Tulasi, G., Author and Digumarti Bhaskara Rao, Editor (2004). *Methods of Teaching Elementary Science.* New Delhi: Discovery Publishing House. ISBN 81-7141-871-6.

Pala Prasada Rao, V., Author and K.N. Rani and D. Bhaskara Rao, Editors (2004). *India Pakistan: Partition Perspectives in Indo-English Novels.* New Delhi: Discovery Publishing House. ISBN 81-7141-871-6.

Pala Prasada Rao, V., Author and D. Bhaskara Rao, Editors (2008). *Functioning of Autonomous Colleges.* New Delhi: Discovery Publishing House Pvt. Ltd. ISBN 978-81-8356-258-4.

Pitchi Reddy, M., Author and Digumarti Bhaskara Rao, Editor (2007). *Techniques of Teaching Social Sciences.* New Delhi: Sonali Publications. ISBN 81-8411-066-X.

Prasad Babu, B., Author and P. Madhu and Digumarti Bhaskara Rao, Editors (2006). *Psychological Adjustment and Well-being.* New Delhi: Discovery Publishing House. ISBN 81-8356-204-3.

Prasad Babu, B., Author and M.V.R. Raju and Digumarti Bhaskara Rao, Editors (2006). *Behavioural Problems of School Children.* New Delhi: Discovery Publishing House. ISBN 81-8356-206-X.

Prabhakaram, K.S., Author and Digumarti Bhaskara Rao, Editors (1998). *Concept Attainment Model in Mathematics Teaching.* New Delhi: Discovery Publishing House. ISBN 81-7141-424-9.

Prasanth Kumar, J., Author and Digumarti Bhaskara Rao, Editor (1998). *Effectiveness of Distance Education System.* New Delhi: Discovery Publishing House. ISBN 81-7141-437-0.

Prasanth Kumar, J., Author and Digumarti Bhaskara Rao, Editor (2004). *Methods of Teaching Civics.* New Delhi: Discovery Publishing House. ISBN 81-7141-806-6.

Prasanth Kumar, J., Author and G. Sundara Rao and Digumarti Bhaskara Rao, Editors (2000). *Open University Student Support Services.* New Delhi: Discovery Publishing House. ISBN 81-7141-550-4.

Raja Kumari, M.A. and D.R.S. Sundari, Authors and Digumarti Bhaskara Rao, Editor (2004). *Special Education.* New Delhi: Discovery Publishing House. ISBN 81-7141-846-5.

Raja Kumari, M.A. and D.R.S. Sundari, Authors and Digumarti Bhaskara Rao, Editor (2004). *Methods of Teaching Educational Psychology.* New Delhi: Discovery Publishing House. ISBN 81-7141-820-1.

Rajeswari, S. M., Author and T. Santhanam, B. Prasad Babu and Digumarti Bhaskara Rao, Editors (2008). *Stress and Attitude of Women Teachers*. New Delhi: Discovery Publishing House Pvt. Ltd. ISBN 978-81-8356-324-6.

Ramatulasamma, K., Author and Digumarti Bhaskara Rao, Editor (2002). *Job Satisfaction of Teacher Educators*. New Delhi: Discovery Publishing House. ISBN 81-7141-655-1.

Rama Krishnaiah, D., Author and Digumarti Bhaskara Rao, Editor (1998). *Job Satisfaction of College Teachers*. New Delhi: Discovery Publishing House. ISBN 81-7141-438-9.

Rama Kumar Ratnam, M.V., Author and Digumarti Bhaskara Rao, Editor (1998). *Dukkha: Suffering in Early Buddhism*. New Delhi: Discovery Publishing House. ISBN 81-7141-653-5.

Rama Krishna Prasad and P. Vide Sagar, Authors and Digumarti Bhaskara Rao, Editor (2004). *Methods of Teaching Physical Education*. New Delhi: Discovery Publishing House. ISBN 81-7141-868-6.

Rama Seshaiah, P. Author and Digumarti Bhaskara Rao, Editor (2004). *Methods of Teaching Home Science*. New Delhi: Discovery Publishing House. ISBN 81-7141-916-X.

Rama Swamy, K., Author and Digumarti Bhaskara Rao, Editor (2007). *Techniques of Teaching Environmental Science*. New Delhi: Sonali Publications. ISBN 81-8411-035-9.

Ramesh, A.R., Author and Digumarti Bhaskara Rao, Editor (2006). *Techniques of Teaching Commerce*. New Delhi: Sonali Publications. ISBN 81-8411-043-X.

Ramesh, Ghanta and Digumarti Bhaskara Rao, Editors (1998). *Environmental Education: Problems and Prospects*. New Delhi: Discovery Publishing House. ISBN 81-7141-423-0.

Ranga Rao, B., Author and Digumarti Bhaskara Rao, Editor (2007). *Techniques of Teaching Economics*. New Delhi: Sonali Publications. ISBN 81-8411-056-1.

Ranga Rao, R., Author and Digumarti Bhaskara Rao, Editor (2004). *Methods of Teacher Teaching*. New Delhi: Discovery Publishing House. ISBN 81-7141-812-0.

Rani, S.S., Author and Digumarti Bhaskara Rao, Editor (2006). *Techniques of Teaching Botany*. New Delhi: Sonali Publications. ISBN 81-8411-037-5.

Rathaiah, Lavu and Digumarti Bhaskara Rao, Editors (1996), *International Innovations in Education*. New Delhi: Discovery Publishing House. ISBN 81-7141-359-5.

Rathaiah, Lavu and Digumarti Bhaskara Rao (1997). *Achievement Correlates*. New Delhi: Discovery Publishing House. ISBN 81-7141-385-4.

Ravi Krishna, M., Author and Digumarti Bhaskara Rao, Editor (2004). *Examination System*. New Delhi: Discovery Publishing House. ISBN 81-7141-824-4.

Ravi Kumar, M., Author and Digumarti Bhaskara Rao, Editor (2004). *Methods of Teaching Computer Science*. New Delhi: Discovery Publishing House. ISBN 81-7141-823-6.

Roja Ramani, V., Author and Digumarti Bhaskara Rao, Editor (2008). *Frustration of Prospective Teachers*. New Delhi: Discovery Publishing House Pvt. Ltd.

Rudramamba, B., Author and Digumarti Bhaskara Rao, Editor (2003). *Problems of Teaching*. New Delhi: APH Publishing Corporation. ISBN 81-7648-462-8.

Rudramamba, B. and V. Lakshmi Kumari, Authors and Digumarti Bhaskara Rao, Editor (2004). *Methods of Teaching Economics*. New Delhi: Discovery Publishing House. ISBN 81-7141-900-3.

Sambasiva Rao, P., Author and Digumarti Bhaskara Rao, Editor (2007). *Techniques of Teaching Psychology*. New Delhi: Sonali Publications. ISBN 81-8411-040-5.

Sanjeeva Rao, P.C., Author and Digumarti Bhaskara Rao, Editor (1996). *A Text Book of Geology*. New Delhi: Discovery Publishing House. ISBN 81-7141-313-7.

Santhanam, T., B. Prasad Babu and S. Sugandhi, Authors and Digumarti Bhaskara Rao, Editor (2007). *Children with Learning Disabilities*. New Delhi: Sonali Publications. ISBN 81-8411-077-4.

Santhanam, T., B. Prasad Babu and S. Sugandhi, Authors and Digumarti Bhaskara Rao, Editor (2008). *Learning Disabilities and Remedial Programmes*. New Delhi: Discovery Publishing House.

Sarala, M.M.O., Author and Digumarti Bhaskara Rao, Editor (2006). *Techniques of Teaching English*. New Delhi: Sonali Publications. ISBN 81-8411-047-2.

Satya Narayana, G., Author and Digumarti Bhaskara Rao, Editor (2008). *Attitude Towards Social Studies and Achievement in Social Studies*. New Delhi: Discovery Publishing House Pvt. Ltd. ISBN 978-81-8356-261-4.

Satya Narayana, V., Author and Digumarti Bhaskara Rao, Editor (2001). *Physical Education, Social Attitudes and Leadership Qualities*. New Delhi: Discovery Publishing House. ISBN 81-7141-593-8.

Satya Narayana, P.V.V. and G. Krishna, Authors and Digumarti Bhaskara Rao, Editor (2004). *Curriculum Development and Management*. New Delhi: Discovery Publishing House. ISBN 81-7141-813-9.

Shamsuddin, Sk. and V. Dayakara Reddy, Authors and Digumarti Bhaskara Rao, Editor (2007). *Academic Achievement and Values*. New Delhi: Discovery Publishing House.

Singh, Y.C., Author and Digumarti Bhaskara Rao, Editor (2006). *Techniques of Teaching Science*. New Delhi: Sonali Publications. ISBN 81-8411-041-3.

Sirisha Rani, S., Author and Digumarti Bhaskara Rao, Editor (2007). *Techniques of Teaching Botany*. New Delhi: Sonali Publications. ISBN 81-8411-037-5.

Sivaratnam Reddy, M., Author and Digumarti Bhaskara Rao, Editor (2004). *Creativity in College Students*. New Delhi: Discovery Publishing House. ISBN 81-7141-697-7.

Siva Lakshmi, G.V. and G.L. Subbaiah, Authors and Digumarti Bhaskara Rao, Editor (2004). *Methods of Teaching Environmental Science*. New Delhi: Discovery Publishing House. ISBN 81-7141-839-2.

Srinivas, G. and Digumarti Bhaskara Rao (2007). *Anxiety of Prospective Teachers.* New Delhi: Sonali Publications. ISBN 81-8411-084-7.

Srinivas, M. and I. Prasada Rao, Authors and Digumarti Bhaskara Rao, Editor (2004). *Methods of Teaching History.* New Delhi: Discovery Publishing House. ISBN 81-7141-803-1.

Srinivas Rao, P., Author and Digumarti Bhaskara Rao, Editor (2007). *Principles of Secondary School.* New Delhi: Sonali Publications. ISBN 81-8411-058-8.

Srinivasulu Reddy, M. and K.R.S. Sambasiva Rao, Authors and Digumarti Bhaskara Rao, Editor (1999). *A Text Book of Aquaculture.* New Delhi: Discovery Publishing House. ISBN 81-7141-482-6.

Srinivasa Rao, Mandalapu, Author and Digumarti Bhaskara Rao, Editor (2003). *Achievement Motivation and Achievement in Mathematics.* New Delhi: Discovery Publishing House. ISBN 81-7141-674-8.

Srihari, M., Author and Digumarti Bhaskara Rao, Editor (2003). *Values of Prospective Teachers.* New Delhi: Discovery Publishing House. ISBN 81-8356-328-7.

Subba Rao, K., Author and Digumarti Bhaskara Rao, Editor (2007). *School Education Policy.* New Delhi: Discovery Publishing House. ISBN 81-8356-285-X.

Subba Rao, K., Author and Digumarti Bhaskara Rao, Editor (2007). *Educational Planning.* New Delhi: Sonali Publications. ISBN 81-8411-053-7.

Sudhakar Reddy, Y., Author and Digumarti Bhaskara Rao, Editor (2003). *Creativity in Adolescents.* New Delhi: Discovery Publishing House. ISBN 81-7141-659-4.

Sunil Kumar, K. and K. Rama Krishana, Authors and Digumarti Bhaskara Rao, Editor (2004). *Methods of Teaching Chemistry.* New Delhi: Discovery Publishing House. ISBN 81-7141-913-5.

Suneetha, G., Author and Digumarti Bhaskara Rao, Editor (2004). *Environmental Awareness of School Students*. New Delhi: Sonali Publications. ISBN 81-8411-085-5.

Sunita, E. and R. Sambasiva Rao, Authors and Digumarti Bhaskara Rao, Editor (2004). *Methods of Teaching Mathematics*. New Delhi: Discovery Publishing House. ISBN 81-7141-915-1.

Suresh, K., Author and Digumarti Bhaskara Rao, Editor (2008). *Social Intelligence of Student Teachers*. New Delhi: Sonali Publications.

Surya Madhava, I., Author and Digumarti Bhaskara Rao, Editor (2006). *Techniques of Teaching Geography*. New Delhi: Sonali Publications. ISBN 81-8411-034-0.

Surya Madhava, I., Author and Digumarti Bhaskara Rao, Editor (2007). *Techniques of Teaching Political Science*. New Delhi: Sonali Publications. ISBN 81-8411-061-8.

Suvarna Raju, T.J.M., Author and M.V.R. Raju, B. Prasad Babu and Digumarti Bhaskara Rao, Editors (2008). *Personality and Adjustment of University Hostel Students*. New Delhi: Sonali Publications.

Swamy, K.R., Author and Digumarti Bhaskara Rao, Editor (2006). *Techniques of Teaching Environmental Science*. New Delhi: Sonali Publications. ISBN 81-8411-035-9.

Swarna Jyothi, K., Author and Digumarti Bhaskara Rao, Editor (2007). *Educational Research*. New Delhi: Sonali Publications. ISBN 81-8411-063-4.

Swarna Latha, C.D., and Digumarti Bhaskara Rao, Editors (2006). *Encyclopaedia of Biotechnology*, 5 Volumes. New Delhi: Discovery Publishing House. ISBN 81-8356-168-3.

Swarupa Rani, T. and J.R. Priyadarshini, Authors and Digumarti Bhaskara Rao, Editor (2004). *Educational Measurement and Evaluation*. New Delhi: Discovery Publishing House. ISBN 81-7141-859-7.

Vanaja, M., Author and Digumarti Bhaskara Rao, Editor (1999). *Inquiry Training Model*. New Delhi: Discovery Publishing House. ISBN 81-7141-515-6.

Vanaja, M., Author and Digumarti Bhaskara Rao, Editor (2004). *Methods of Teaching Physics*. New Delhi: Discovery Publishing House. ISBN 81-7141-867-8.

Valeri V. Koustiouk, Author and Digumarti Bhaskara Rao, Editor (2002). *A Text Book of Cryogenics*. New Delhi: Discovery Publishing House. ISBN 81-7141-642-X.

Vamsi Krishna, V., Author and Digumarti Bhaskara Rao, Editor (2004). *School Psychology*. New Delhi: Discovery Publishing House. ISBN 81-7141-880-5.

Veena Kumari, Balusu and Digumarti Bhaskara Rao (1996). *Operation Black Board*. New Delhi: APH Publishing Corporation. ISBN 81-7024-711-X.

Veena Kumari, Balusu, Author and Digumarti Bhaskara Rao, Editor (2004). *Methods of Teaching Social Studies*. New Delhi: Discovery Publishing House. ISBN 81-7141-899-6.

Veena Kumari, Balusu, Author and Digumarti Bhaskara Rao, Editor (2000). *Psycho-Social Correlates of Achievement*. New Delhi: Discovery Publishing House. ISBN 81-7141-547-4.

Venkata Rao, B., Author and Digumarti Bhaskara Rao, Editor (2007). *Techniques of Teaching Chemistry*. New Delhi: Sonali Publications. ISBN 81-8411-057-X.

Venkata Rao, P. and Digumarti Bhaskara Rao (1989). *A Text Book of Zoology—Junior Intermediate*. Guntur: Vignan Publishers.

Venkata Rao, P. and Digumarti Bhaskara Rao (1989). *A Text Book of Zoology—Senior Intermediate*. Guntur: Vignan Publishers.

Venkateswara Rao, V., Author and Digumarti Bhaskara Rao, Editor (2004). *Problems of Education*. New Delhi: Discovery Publishing House. ISBN 81-7141-841-4.

Venkateswara Rao, V., V. Vijaya Lakshmi and V. Vamsi Krishna, Authors and Digumarti Bhaskara Rao, Editor (2004). *Education For All.* New Delhi: Sonali Publications. ISBN 81-88836-30-3.

Venkateswara Rao, V., V. Vijaya Lakshmi and V. Vamsi Krishna, Authors and Digumarti Bhaskara Rao, Editor (2004). *Education in India.* New Delhi: Sonali Publications. ISBN 81-88836-858-9.

Venkateswara Reddy, L. and Narayana, M.L., Authors and Digumarti Bhaskara Rao, Editor (2004). *Education for Dalits.* New Delhi: Discovery Publishing House. ISBN 81-7141-872-4.

Venkateswara Reddy, L. and Narayana, M. L, Authors and Digumarti Bhaskara Rao, Editor (2004). *Methods of Teaching Rural Sociology.* New Delhi: Discovery Publishing House. ISBN 81-7141-811-2.

Venkateswarlu, K. and S.J. Basha, Authors and Digumarti Bhaskara Rao, Editor (2004). *Methods of Teaching Commerce.* New Delhi: Discovery Publishing House. ISBN 81-7141-808-2.

Venugopala Rao, K., Author and Digumarti Bhaskara Rao, Editor (2000). *Teacher Morale in Secondary Schools.* New Delhi: Discovery Publishing House. ISBN 81-7141-551-2.

Venugopala Rao, K., Author and Digumarti Bhaskara Rao, Editor (2007). *Techniques of Teaching History.* New Delhi: Sonali Publications. ISBN 81-8411-059-6.

Vidya, C., Author and Digumarti Bhaskara Rao, Editor (1996). *A Text Book of Nutrition.* New Delhi: Discovery Publishing House. ISBN 81-7141-309-9.

Vimala, T.D., B. Prasad Babu and Digumarti Bhaskara Rao, Editors (2007). *Stress, Coping and Management.* New Delhi: Sonali Publications. ISBN 81-8411-086-3.

Vijaya Bharathi, D., Author and Digumarti Bhaskara Rao, Editor (2000). *Educational Philosophies of Swami Vivekananda and John Dewey.* New Delhi: APH Publishing House. ISBN 81-7648-309-9.

Vijaya Bharathi, D., Author and Digumarti Bhaskara Rao, Editor (2005). *Educational Philosophy of John Dewey*. New Delhi: Discovery Publishing House. ISBN 81-8356-024-5.

Vijaya Bharathi, D., Author and Digumarti Bhaskara Rao, Editor (2005). *Educational Philosophy of Swami Vivekananda*. New Delhi: Discovery Publishing House. ISBN 81-8356-023-7.

Vijaya Lakshmi, D., Author and Digumarti Bhaskara Rao, Editor (2004) *Basic Education*. New Delhi: Discovery Publishing House. ISBN 81-7141-881-3.

Vijaya Lakshmi, V., Author and Digumarti Bhaskara Rao, Editor (2006). *Techniques of Teaching Music*. New Delhi: Sonali Publications. ISBN 81-8411-038-3.

Vijaya Kumar, S.J., Author and Digumarti Bhaskara Rao, Editor (2006). *Techniques of Teaching Mathematics*. New Delhi: Sonali Publications. ISBN 81-8411-039-1.

Visalakshi, V., Author and Digumarti Bhaskara Rao, Editor (2006). *Techniques of Teaching Biology*. New Delhi: Sonali Publications. ISBN 81-8411-045-6.

Visalakshi, V., Author and Digumarti Bhaskara Rao, Editor (2007). *Techniques of Teaching Zoology*. New Delhi: Sonali Publications. ISBN 81-8411-055-3.

Books in Telugu Language

Bhaskara Rao, Digumarti (1986). *Dhrushya Sravana Bodhanapakaranalu* (Audio Visual Teaching Aids). Guntur: Nagarjuna Publishers.

Bhaskara Rao, Digumarti (1993). *Jeevasasthra Bodhana* (Teaching of Biology). Guntur: Nagarjuna Publishers.

Bhaskara Rao, Digumarti (1995). *Vignanasasthra Bodhana* (Teaching of science) Guntur: Nagarjuna Publishers.

Bhaskara Rao, Digumarti (1997). *Vidya Manovignana Sasthram* (Educational Psychology). Guntur: Creative Press.

Bhaskara Rao, Digumarti (1998). *DSC Study Material*. Guntur: Nagarjuna Publishers.

Bhaskara Rao, Digumarti (1998). *Upadhyayudu Vidya.* (Teacher and Education) Guntur: Nagarjuna Publishers.

Bhaskara Rao, Digumarti (1998). *Vidya Drukpadalu* (Perspectives of Education). Guntur: Nagarjuna Publishers.

Bhaskara Rao, Digumarti (1999). *EdCET Teaching Aptitude.* Guntur: Nagarjuna Publishers.

Bhaskara Rao, Digumarti (2001). *Bharata Samajamulo Upadyayudu Vidhya* (Teacher and Education in Emerging Indian Society). Guntur: Sri Nagarjuna Publishers.

Bhaskara Rao, Digumarti (2001). *Bhoutika Sasthra Bodhana Padhatulu* (Methods of Teaching Physical Science). Guntur: Sri Nagarjuna Publishers.

Bhaskara Rao, Digumarti (2001). *Jeeva Sasthra Bodhana Padhatulu* (Methods of Teaching Biology). Guntur: Sri Nagarjuna Publishers.

Bhaskara Rao, Digumarti (2001). *Vidya Manovignana Sasthram* (Educational Psychology). Guntur: Sri Nagarjuna Publishers.

Bhaskara Rao, Digumarti (2003). *Patasala Yajamanyam / Paripalana* (School Management and Administration). Guntur: Sri Nagarjuna Publishers.

Gopala Krishna, G., A. Rama Krishna, K. Subba Rao and Bhaskara Rao, Digumarti (2004). *Jeevasasthra Bodhana Padhatulu* (Methods of Teaching of Biological Science). Guntur: Sri Nagarjuna Publishers.

Krishna Murthy, V., K.S. Sudheer Reddy and Digumarti Bhaskara Rao (2004). *Vidya Manovignana Sasthra Adharalu* (Foundations of Educational Psychology). Guntur: Sri Nagarjuna Publishers.

Lalini, V., V. Dayakara Reddy, M. Srihari and Digumarti Bhaskara Rao (2004). *Vidya Adharalu* (Foundations of Education). Guntur: Sri Nagarjuna Publishers.

Subba Rao, K.P., P. Ayodhya and Digumarti Bhaskara Rao (2004). *Patasala Yajamanyam – Vidhya Vyavasthalu* (School Management and Systems of Education). Guntur: Sri Nagarjuna Publishers.

Sudhakar, V., B. Ravindra Babu, D.S. Kumar and Digumarti Bhaskara Rao (2004). *Vidya Sanketika Sasthram—Computer Vidhya* (Educational Technology and Computer Education). Guntur: Sri Nagarjuna Publishers.

Index

W

❑❑❑